Singing the Mercies of the Lord
Writings on Saint Thérèse of Lisieux

by

Brian J. Nolan

Celebrating the 100th Anniversary of Her Canonization

Edited by Simon Nolan, O. Carm.

Carmelite Media

This book was originally published as a series of articles

Layout and Cover design by William J. Harry, O. Carm.

Second Edition

Carmelite Media
8501 Bailey Road
Darien, Illinois 60561

Phone: 1-630-971-0724
Email: publications@carmelnet.org
Website: carmelites.info/publications

Printed Book ISBN: 978-1-936742-33-2
eBook ISBN: 978-1-936742-34-9

I shall begin to sing what I must sing eternally:

"The Mercies of the Lord" (Psalm 88:2)

Saint Thérèse of Lisieux
Manuscript A
January 1895

Contents

IV. Saint Thérèse, Ireland, and Other Places

V. Saint Thérèse and the Theatre

Introduction

This book is a timely publication in a year of anniversaries associated with Saint Thérèse of Lisieux: the 150th anniversary of her birth in 1873 and the 100th anniversary of her beatification by Pope Pius XI in 1923.

Brian J. Nolan (1943-2018) lived and worked in Dublin, Ireland, and studied theology at Trinity College, Dublin and at St Patrick's College, Maynooth. Proficient in biblical as well as modern languages, he completed a research degree at Trinity on the Book of Leviticus under the direction of Professor A.C.C. Mayes and another at Maynooth on the notion of abandonment in Saint Thérèse of Lisieux under the direction of Professor Bede McGregor, OP. He taught theology for a number of years at Dublin's Milltown Institute of Theology and Philosophy. He published extensively, particularly on the spirituality of Saint Thérèse of Lisieux but also on the English mystics and the Irish saints, in *Spirituality*, *Mount Carmel*, and *Carmel in the World*. His son, Fr Simon Nolan, O. Carm., who holds a doctoral degree from Rome's Pontifical Gregorian University and who has edited this volume, is Dean of the Faculty of Philosophy at Maynooth and Prior of Whitefriar Street Carmelite Church and Priory in Dublin. He is also a Scholar at the Center for Carmelite Studies at the Catholic University of America, Washington, DC.

True to the origins of this book in individual articles published in the pages of various journals of spirituality, chapters may be read as separate units. At times a small amount of repetition of theme and content is discernible; there has been no attempt to edit this out. Referencing, in keeping with the popular level at which most of the original articles were written, is not exhaustive, but has, nevertheless, been standardised across chapters and added in the small number of cases where original articles had none.

This book is dedicated to the memory of Brian Nolan and to his wife, Monica, sons, Simon and Garrett, and daughter, Sarah.

Profound gratitude is expressed to Fr Yamai Bature, OCD, editor of *Mount Carmel*, for permission to reprint chapters 4, 8, 13, 14, 18, 19, 22, 23, 24; to Fr PJ Breen, editor of *Carmel in the World*, for permission to reprint chapters 3, 16, 17, 25; to Fr Tom Jordan, OP, editor of *Spirituality*, for permission to reprint chapters 1, 2, 6, 7, 9, 10, 11, 15, 20, 26; to Fr Donal Neary, SJ, Messenger Publications, Dublin, for permission to reprint chapter 5; to Dominican Publications, Dublin, for permission to reprint chapters 12 and 21.

The editor expresses his gratitude to those who initially planted the seed of the idea of gathering his father's articles into book form: Fr Michael McGoldrick, OCD, Fr Richard Byrne, O. Carm., Fr Tom Jordan, OP, Ms Joanne Mosley, and the late Mr Pat Sweeney. Thanks are due also to Fr Dave Twohig, O. Carm., for his assistance with a number of texts.

However, the strongest expression of gratefulness is due to Fr William J. Harry, O. Carm., of Carmelite Media for supporting this project from start to finish. Without his patience and encouragement this book would never have seen the light of day.

Simon Nolan, O. Carm.
Carmelite Priory
Whitefriar Street, Dublin
Solemnity of Our Lady of Mount Carmel, July 16th, 2023

I

Saint Thérèse and Her Sisters

Chapter One

'Saint Thérèse of the Child Jesus': The Origin and Significance of Her Religious Name

Nine-year-old Thérèse was overjoyed when Mother Marie de Gonzague, the then prioress of the local Carmel in Lisieux, proposed the very religious name she desired when she too became a Carmelite like her sister Pauline, whom she was visiting: 'Sister Thérèse of the Child Jesus.' She regarded this "happy meeting of minds" as a special favour from the Divine Infant. Four years later, she would also attribute her 'Christmas conversion' to "the gentle, *little* Child of only one hour" when she suddenly recovered from the hypersensitivity that had afflicted her since her mother died when she was a four and a half: "He made strong and courageous"[1] Thérèse had always wished that nature would be adorned in white just as she would be on the day she took the habit, January 10, 1889. When she entered the cloister, as if on cue, the first thing that struck her as she was "the little Jesus...smiling at her."[2] This is a reference to the statue of the Rose Child Jesus she loved to adorn, and with which she is photographed during community recreation. Her glance was then immediately drawn to the monastery garden behind the statue covered under a blanket of snow, the result of an unexpected snowfall that surprised the entire people of Lisieux.

The Rose Child Jesus was but one of several different images of the Divine Infant in the convent. For example, Thérèse stopped each day to pray before a statue of the Infant of Prague close to

---

1. St Thérèse of Lisieux, *Story of a Soul*, trans. J. Clarke, Washington DC: ICS Publications, 1996, p. 97.

2. *Ibid.*, p. 155. For an account and photographs of the Rose Child Jesus, see Pierre Descouvemont & Helmuth Nils Loose, *Thérèse and Lisieux*, Dublin: Veritas, 1996, pp. 132-133; for an account and images of other mentioned statues, Lisieux crib, 'coat of arms', and prayer cards, see pp. 156-163.

her cell. This devotion was spread throughout the world by the Discalced Carmelite friars, after the widowed Bohemian Princess Polyxena entrusted the statue to them for the benefit of all the faithful in 1683. Devotion to the Holy Child is a means of honouring Jesus in the Incarnation, the mystery of the Word made flesh. It has expressed itself in different ways across the world ever since the Lord's birth. The adoration continued among Church Fathers and saints in later centuries, for example Francis of Assisi who gave us the crib. Such has been the warmth and universality of the devotion to the Child Jesus that it has been the subject of works by many famous artists, writers and poets. The popularity of the devotion has also given rise to a wonderful array of statues, sometimes in sumptuous attire.

Céline, Sr Geneviève of the Holy Face, the closest sister and confidante of Thérèse, points out, "it was the Mystery of the Infant Jesus in the crib at Bethlehem that was [Thérèse's] special delight."[3] This piety is reflected, for example, in Thérèse's prayers and poetry; her delight in writing plays for the feast of the Nativity, and the cutting of the white velvet dress she wore on the day she took the habit to provide the bedding and tunic for the Divine Infant doll in the convent crib; the doll's hair being cut from her own hair which had been kept since she was a child. Two years before she died she would also often write out the profound thought that 'A God who makes Himself so little can only be love and mercy.' This sentiment echoes her liberating insight into the divine mercy that freed her from the great anguish she suffered during her early years in Carmel from an extreme dread of sin; and led to the discovery of her celebrated spiritual doctrine The Little Way which teaches us how to joyfully accept our flawed human nature and to look upon our sins in a more positive light.

Yet another statue in the convent at Lisieux was that of the Child Jesus of the Carmel of Beaune, associated with the seventeenth century nun Sister Margaret of the Blessed Sacrament, to whom the Child Jesus appeared. It was before this statue that Pauline encouraged Thérèse to append 'the Holy Face' to her precious religious name. By initiating Thérèse into this piety Pauline was following the custom of the saintly foundress of the Lisieux Carmel, Mother

---

3. Sr Geneviève of the Holy Face (Céline Martin), *My Sister Saint Thérèse*, Rockford, Illinois: Tan Books, 1897, p. 47.

Geneviève of Saint Teresa. Pauline told her young sister, that among other things "…the disfigured face of the suffering Saviour would encourage her to live in humility and to remain well hidden…"[4] Thus, when Thérèse meditated before the Holy Face she would use the suffering servant readings from the prophet Isaiah and "…desired to be without beauty, alone in treating the wine press, unknown to everyone."[5] The Holy Face not only became central to Thérèse's piety but further intensified at the time her father Louis Martin[6] became mentally ill in 1888. Years later she would realise that a mysterious vision she had as a child was a prophecy of her beloved father's illness: she had seen a man exactly like her father with a cloth hiding his face in the garden beneath an attic window. She compared her father's humiliation with the Passion of Jesus and linked it with her Holy Face devotion. Céline testified that the devotion of her closest sister and confidante to the Holy Face "…transcended or more accurately embraced – all the other attractions of her spiritual life."[7] This priority is reflected, for example, in Thérèse painting the image on vestments and pictures; making holy cards adorned with her own art work; encouraging her novices to add the Holy Face to their name, and the image features in most of her important poems and some of her prayers between 1896 and the beginning of 1897.

Devotion to the Holy Face has its origins in the veneration of the veil of St Veronica with its imprint of the Holy Face of Jesus, now kept in the Vatican. It was venerated in Rome as early as 610. Popular devotion to the Holy Face continued in later centuries in varying degrees. One notable time of revival took place in France in 1845 when it was revealed by Our Lord to a nun in the Carmel of Tours, Sister Marie of Saint-Pierre (1816-1848), that he would imprint his features on the souls of all those who venerated his Holy Face in reparation for blasphemy and other outrages. The devotion was further promoted by Leon Dupont, later known as the holy man of Tours and now declared Venerable. Many devotees

---

4. Descouvemont & Loose, *op. cit.*, p. 137.

5. *Last Conversations*, ed. J. Clarke, Washington, DC: ICS Publications, 1977, p. 135.

6. Thérèse's parents Louis and Azélie-Marie (Zélie) Martin were canonized as saints by Pope Francis on 18th October 2015.

7. Sr Geneviève of the Holy Face (Céline Martin), *My Sister Saint Thérèse*, Rockford, Illinois: Tan Books, 1897, p. 111.

came to this house where he kept a light burning day and night before a picture of the Holy Face. On April 26, 1885, Thérèse's father enrolled himself and his five daughters in the Confraternity at the suggestion of Pauline.

Contrary to how it may appear at first sight, there is nothing odd about Pauline having suggested the Holy Face devotion to Thérèse before a statue of the Child Jesus, or with linking the two devotions together in her religious name. As Thérèsian scholar Bishop Guy Gaucher explains, "far from being in opposition–the Child Jesus and the Suffering Christ–they are deeply united. It is one and the same person. From childhood he knew suffering; naked on the straw of the cave, pursued by men, fleeing from Egypt."[8] This unity was reflected in popular French piety in which the association of the Child Jesus with his suffering was widely evident in popular holy pictures depicting the infant Jesus with the cross or crown of thorns. Thérèse was given one such card by one of her novices Sister Martha to mark her reception of the veil on September 24, 1890. This image is thought to have given Thérèse the idea for her painting *The Dream of the Child Jesus* in which the Divine Infant dreams about his Passion. And to have suggested the idea for Thérèse's Christmas play in 1895 *The Divine Little Beggar* in which the community were invited to offer their love to "the Infant hidden in swaddling clothes…who can nevertheless suffer."[9] The close association of the Divine Child with Calvary goes back further still having been a favourite contemplation of Cardinal Pierre de Bérulle (1575-1629) the founder of the French School of Spirituality.

While Thérèse's devotion to the Holy Face became of prime importance to her in Carmel, both devotions continued to the end of her life. Moreover, their significance as a unity in her religious name grew in significance. This development is already evident in her 'wedding invitation', at the time of her profession, in which she describes her religious names as titles of nobility and the dowry of her Divine Spouse.[10] In January 1896, the year before she died

8. G. Gaucher, *The Passion of Thérèse of Lisieux*, Homebush: St. Paul Communications, 1989, p. 227.

9. *The Plays of St Thérèse of Lisieux*, trans. S. Conroy & D. Dwyer, Washington DC: ICS Publications, 2008, p. 231.

10. See *Letters of St Thérèse of Lisieux*, trans. J. Clarke, Washington DC: ICS Publications, vol.2, p. 679.

at 24, the importance of her complete religious identity is again made clear on her 'coat of arms' depicting images of both the Child Jesus and the Holy Face. Possibly dating from a retreat in September 7-18, 1896, she made a card with four prayers for her breviary using photos of the Child Jesus of Messine[11] and the Holy Face of Tours taken by Céline. In her important analysis of the prayers, Alethia Kane finds the prayer card to be "a type of identity card summing up [Thérèse's] religious name. She has a strong sense of its meaning as completing and defining her baptismal name. Your name is your mission she writes as far back as 1890 (Letter 109)."[12] Finally, on June 7, 1897, a few months before she died, an exhausted Thérèse would go to great pains to pose before Céline's camera while holding the Messine and Tours pictures "to leave a visual testament of her religious name, which sums up her vocation and her 'mission'."[13]

---

11. So-called because her novice and friend Sr Marie of the Trinity brought the picture with her when she was transferred to Lisieux from the Paris Carmel on l'avenue Messine.

12. *The Prayers of St. Thérèse of Lisieux*, trans. A. Kane O.C.D., Washington DC: ICS Publications, 1977, p. 105.

13. *Ibid.*, pp. 19-20.

Chapter Two

The True Freedom of Marie Martin

Marie Martin (1860–1940) was the first-born of Saints Louis and Zélie Martin's nine children, only five of whom survived into adulthood, all of them girls. She also has the distinction of being the godmother of her youngest sister Saint Thérèse, and of playing an important role in her spiritual and educational formation. In addition, Marie was the catalyst behind Thérèse's autobiographical spiritual classic *Story of a Soul*. Moreover, it was she who asked Thérèse to express her thoughts on the Blessed Virgin in writing, resulting in the saint's most beautiful poem *Why I Love You Mary*. Marie's loving care of Thérèse, after their mother died, resulted in her being one of the most important witnesses at her youngest sister's beatification process, especially concerning the saint's healing from a mysterious illness before the statue now known as Our Lady of the Smile. For these reasons alone, we might understandably wish to enquire further into Marie's life. But the eldest Martin girl is interesting for other reasons too, not least her discovery of true liberty.

Marie was somewhat eccentric and had a remarkable spirit of independence that manifested itself in various ways, sometimes disconcertingly so. For example, she found the then custom of curtsying before people demeaning and bluntly told her mother: "It does not matter whether people like me or not. So long as you love me, that is enough."[1]

Marie had an intense dislike for following the crowd and refused to bow to the demands of fashion. She detested putting on a new dress and did not use make-up. Although she went to mass daily she had an aversion to certain traditional forms of piety, and would

---

1. Stéphane-Joseph Piat, O.F.M., *The Story of a Family: The Home of St Thérèse of Lisieux*, Rockford, Illinois: Tan Books, 1994, p. 189.

flinch at the very suggestion of a religious vocation, as indeed she did marriage.

Marie's autonomy and eccentricity resulted in her being called various affectionate nicknames such as the "Lioness of Jesus." There was one notable exception however. When Marie used her own frequently used expression "I am quite free" to boldly defend herself against the sharp tongue of the domineering family maid Louise, the latter unkindly turned it into a nickname against her: "I-am-quite-free." However, the spontaneity of Marie was poetically remembered by her observant youngest sister Thérèse, who was thirteen years her junior:

> Of old, I saw her in her independence,
> Seeking true happiness in freedom wide.[2]

In October 1868, eight-year-old Marie, and Pauline, seven, were sent to the prestigious boarding school at the Visitation convent in Le Mans, where their beloved maternal aunt Sr Marie-Dosithée was a teacher. Although she never fully settled there, Marie proved to be a very good student and almost every quarter received the top awards for her scholarly achievements. Most of Marie's companions at the school belonged to the nobility. When she befriended one such girl she became ambitious for their lifestyle. Understandably, Marie's inordinate affection worried her saintly parents, who eschewed luxury despite their success in business. Her mother remarked in a letter to Pauline:

> There is Marie dreaming of going to live in a fine house, opposite the Poor Clares…She talked about it all yesterday evening. One would have thought it was Heaven…Although your sister has so little worldliness about her, she is never content where she is. She is ambitious for something better; she must have beautiful rooms, spacious and well furnished… When she has something different, perhaps she will feel its insufficiency still more.[3]

Marie's mother also became concerned for a while to see her eldest daughter "…systematically hostile to the outward manifestations of religious fervour."[4] However, she did not lose courage and decided

---

2. Quoted in *ibid.*, p. 192.
3. Quoted in *ibid.*, p. 193.
4. *Ibid.*, p. 194.

to send Marie to an 'old girl' retreat at the Visitation convent, as she had at the time of Marie's fascination with grandeur. These and other wise initiatives brought positive results. Eventually, Marie was so transformed that Zélie and her sister Dosithée even shared a secret presentiment that she would become a religious.

Sadly, Zélie and Dosithée both died in 1877. Louis then moved the family from Alençon to Lisieux where he bought a house, which the children named Les Buissonnets. The burden of running the household and teaching duties at the family home fell mainly on the shoulders of seventeen-year-old Marie. She was assisted by Pauline with whom she was very close and united. However, when Pauline departed for Carmel in 1882, Marie was left on her own to fulfil the tasks of stand-in mother and teacher to both Thérèse (9) and Céline (13). And she more than coped. Her mother, having had a presentiment of her own death, had already prepared Marie by making her take her share in the housekeeping upon leaving the school at Le Mans. Thus, for example, when Thérèse was stricken by a mysterious nervous illness in March 25, 1883, Easter Sunday, she expressed gratitude for the tender motherly care Marie lavished on her. And when she suddenly beheld the beautiful countenance of the Blessed Virgin Mary in the following April 13, Pentecost Sunday, she attributed this grace and her healing to the touching motherly prayers of Marie before the statue of the Blessed Virgin: "Ah, it really was to her that I owe the grace of the Queen of Heaven's smile."[5] Marie also proved to be an outstanding godmother to Thérèse. For example, when she helped to prepare Thérèse for her First Communion on 8 May 1884, her godchild was full of praise for her eloquent godmother at this momentous time who "explained the way of becoming holy through fidelity in little things."[6]

In 1886, the autonomy of Marie led her into a completely unexpected place. Having previously dismissed out of hand the prospect of ever becoming a religious, she rendered her family speechless one day by announcing she was going to do just that. She had struggled in vain against the promptings of her Jesuit

5. St Thérèse of Lisieux, *Story of a Soul*, Washington DC: ICS Publications, 1996, p. 66.
6. *Ibid.*, p. 74.

spiritual director, Father Almire Pichon but felt "caught in the nets of divine mercy."[7] Marie followed Pauline into the cloisters of the local Carmel that autumn, leaving seventeen-year-old Céline in charge at home. However, beforehand she had to say a special good-bye to her beloved father Louis, who stifled a sob at the thought of being without his treasured 'diamond': "God could not ask a greater sacrifice from me. I thought you would never leave me."[8] Marie took the religious name that Fr Pichon had chosen for her: Sister Marie of the Sacred Heart.[9] Moreover, he made the long boat journey back to France from Canada, where he had moved two years previously as a missionary, to attend her reception of the habit on 15 October 1886, and to deliver the homily.

It was at Carmel as an enclosed nun that Marie asked Pauline (then Mother Agnès) to order Thérèse to write down the memories of her childhood that resulted in Manuscript A, the first of three texts that formed the *Story of a Soul*. In addition, Marie asked Thérèse directly to write the treasured letter that became Manuscript B, in which the saint exclaims "MY VOCATION IS LOVE!"

Marie proved to be an avid gardener in Carmel. Wearing her favourite canvas apron and large hob-nailed boots, she went about tending the monastery gardens with remarkable tenacity. She was, for example, able to wrest the particularly stubborn couch-grass from the ground, a challenging task that even the regular gardener refused to undertake. Marie's gardening also gave rise to some profound thoughts that resulted in her being charmingly referred to as "Our mystic gardener." For example, she saw herself as a rare flower that God planted in his chosen garden Carmel, who was free to give as much or as little glory to the Divine Gardener as might decide:

> I have desired to be holy that He may derive more joy in contemplating His flower... I understand better than I could ever say, the disinterested love of the elect...Their own glory is nothing to them...It is He alone Whom they love; they forget themselves entirely...[10]

---

7. Piat, *op cit.*, p. 342.

8. *Ibid.*, p. 345.

9. All five Martin daughters entered religious life, four of them as Carmelites: Pauline, Marie, Thérèse and Céline, in that order. Léonie became a Visitation sister.

10. Mother Agnes of Jesus, O.C.D., [Pauline Martin] *Marie, Sister of St Thérèse,*

After Thérèse died on 30 September 1897, when she was 24, Marie was one of the many recipients of her godchild's continuing posthumous visitations to earth, known as the Shower of Roses. She perceived Thérèse to be at her side helping to straighten out her rheumatic limbs, in answer to the prayers of the infirmarian, and on a second occasion she experienced the tender presence of Thérèse tenderly replacing the blanket "…on the numbed shoulders."[11]

When Thérèse discovered her spiritual doctrine, The Little Way, around late 1894-early 1895, Marie mainly depended on it for her inspiration. However, in 1896, when Thérèse asked her if she would like to recite her newly composed Act of Oblation to Merciful Love and become a "holocaust victim" to the love of God, Marie declined the invitation. She was scared to death by the very suggestion because she had a dread of suffering and was also repelled by the word 'victim.' However, Thérèse explained that her offering is in fact a request to be overwhelmed by the tender merciful love of God. She put Marie's mind at rest and her godmother went on to become one of the oblation's greatest advocates. Indeed, Marie is thought to have been reciting the offering when she was dying on 19 January 1940, until she suddenly stopped and raised her head, "…opened her large eyes, filled with light and assurance, glanced upward, and then gazed steadily at the statue of Our Lady of the Smile. Then she bowed her head, and with an expression of peace and joy on her face… expired."[12]

It is a wonderful irony that Marie Martin, who had once recoiled at the very mention of entering religious life, should eventually come to discover true freedom when she became an enclosed nun within the walls of the local Carmelite monastery, with its austere living conditions and routine: "Now that He [Jesus] has drawn me, I find myself behind the grill, the happiest of creatures. I find myself in possession of true liberty, Ah, it is now I can really say: "I am quite free."[13]

---

trans. Fr. Colaresi, O. Carm., see Ch. 3, subtitle 'Marie, the gardener.' This Carmelite obituary letter is now published on the website of the Archives of Lisieux Carmel. Suggested web search: Circular Sr. Marie of the Sacred Heart.

11. *Ibid.*, Ch. 5, under subheading 'Marie's Zeal for the Little Way of Thérese.'

12. *Ibid.*, Ch. 7, under subheading 'Marie's Death.'

13. Quoted in Joseph P. Kochiss, *A Companion to St Thérèse of Lisieux: Her Life and Work and the People and Places in Her Story*, Kettering OH: Angelico Press, 2014, p. 125.

Chapter Three

The Transformation of 'Poor Léonie'

When Léonie Martin was chosen to lead the small funeral procession of her sister Thérèse to the Lisieux town cemetery on October 4, 1897, due to her uncle Isidore Guérin being unwell, it was a fitting turn of events. Thérèse had done so much to turn Léonie's difficult life around by patiently teaching her the liberating insights of her newly discovered spiritual doctrine, The Little Way. Along with most of Thérèse's Carmelite novices at the Lisieux monastery, where she was the *de facto* novice mistress, Léonie was one of the first beneficiaries of her sister's spiritual doctrine.

From the time she was born on June 3, 1863, the odds were stacked against Léonie. The first indication that all was not right is reflected in her mother Zélie's letter to her brother Isidore the following January: '...The poor child is very delicate...'[1] Léonie grew up to be emotionally and intellectually disadvantaged and suffered from a catalogue of health complaints, including a case of purulent eczema. Moreover, her behaviour was often rebellious; generally disruptive and undisciplined. A slow learner, she was quite the opposite of her bright and talented sisters, even in appearance. The death of her closest sister and friend, five-and-a-half-year-old Hélene in 1870 was thought to have possibly affected Léonie psychologically and worsened her difficulty with learning. Referred to as 'Poor Léonie' by her immediate and wider family, she was naturally a constant source of concern for her loving and devout parents.[2] So much so, indeed, when the dying Zélie brought her daughter to Lourdes in June 1877 she prayed more for Léonie than for herself. She was convinced that only a miracle would cure her

---

1. Stéphane-Joseph Piat, O.F.M., *The Story of a Family: The Home of St Thérèse of Lisieux*. Rockford, Illinois: Tan Books. p. 52.

2. Louis and Zélie were the first spouses in the history of the Church to be canonized as a couple on October 18, 2015.

daughter's difficult nature. And she was not without hope. Léonie had already been healed of an unnamed illness from which she should have died when she was only sixteen months old. The child's recovery followed a novena to Blessed Margaret Mary, made by Zélie's sister Marie-Louise (Sister Marie-Dosithée) at her request. Marie-Louise was a Visitation nun and a teacher at their school at Le Mans. She was confident that with the grace of God and hard work even the most intractable natures could be reformed. And she had a considerable influence on Léonie. However, her own efforts to stabilise her niece proved to be something of a challenge. Her disappointment with progress is recorded in a letter to her brother: 'At the moment I am taking care of Léonie that terrible little girl; she certainly keeps me on my toes. It's a continual little battle...'[3] However, she could see that despite Léonie's trying nature her niece was not without redeeming characteristics:

> She is a difficult child to train, and her childhood will not show any attractiveness, but I believe that she will eventually be as good as her sisters. She has a heart of gold, her intelligence is not developed and she is backward for her age. Nevertheless, she does not lack capabilities, and I find that she has good judgement and also a remarkable strength of character...In short, by nature she is strong and generous, quite to my taste. But if the grace of God were not there what would become of her.[4]

Indeed, Marie-Louise believed that one day Léonie would also become a Visitation sister. When Leonie was fourteen her aunt was diagnosed with tuberculosis. In a touching letter, the turbulent rebel of the Martin household made a remarkable request of her dying aunt: she asked Marie-Louise if she would bring a message to Heaven asking God to send her the grace of conversion and a vocation to become a true religious. Asked to clarify what she meant by 'true religious' Léonie replied, 'It means I want to become a very good religious and then a saint.'[5]

Despite these positive signs, a mysterious gulf still divided Léonie from her mother who was now dying from cancer. Zélie was

---

3. Marie Baudouin-Croix, *Léonie Martin: A Difficult Life*. Dublin: Veritas, 1993. p. 17.

4. Joseph P. Kochiss, *A Companion to Saint Thérèse of Lisieux*. Kettering OH: Angelico Press, p. 139.

5. Baudouin-Croix, *op cit.*, p. 25.

understandably concerned about what might happen to Léonie in her absence. She prayed to her deceased sister, Marie-Louise, and asked her to plead Léonie's cause before God. Her prayer was answered when she made the shocking discovery that their cruel housekeeper, Louise Marais, had been taking advantage of her daughter's natural weakness. Astonishingly, Léonie had been beaten and threatened with punishment by the maid if she obeyed her parents and behaved well. Although freed from her enslavement Léonie was still fickle and turbulent. But she was no longer shut into herself. She was now trying hard to mend her ways. The brooding Léonie of old now confided everything to her mother. Indeed, her love for Zélie was so great that she wanted to die in her place. Before Zélie died on August 28, 1877, six months after the demise of her sister Marie-Louise, she predicted that 'Léonie will love God very much, and will be good to everyone.'[6]

Although Léonie showed signs of improvement her transformation was not yet complete. That would only come after years of spiritual struggle under the wise and affectionate guidance of her sister Thérèse. Léonie joined the Poor Clares in Alençon in 1866 where she once prayed with her mother. But she found it too rigorous and left within two months. It was the first of four attempts at entering religious life, having then tried to enter the Visitation order at Caen on three occasions. Eventually, as predicted by Sister Marie-Dosithée, she succeeded with her third attempt on January 8, 1899. Her loving sister Thérèse, who had become her mentor, had died two years earlier on September 30, 1897. Thérèse had accurately predicted that after her death Léonie would finally be successful in entering the Visitation order and that she would take her name and that of St Francis de Sales. Léonie remained at the Visitation convent as Sister Françoise-Thérèse for forty-two years until her death.

During the thirteen years that Léonie took to realise her vocation, her sisters Marie, Thérèse and Céline joined their sister Pauline as enclosed Carmelites in the local Lisieux Carmel. Her saintly father Louis, who had been afflicted with a mental disorder, died on July 29, 1894, after being nursed by Léonie and her sister Céline. During those years Léonie had grown in wisdom having been gently steered towards peace and holiness under the tender guidance of

6. *Ibid.*, p. 32.

Thérèse's Little Way. After Thérèse died Léonie sometimes strongly felt her sister's presence. She told her sister Pauline about one outstanding occasion that occurred in 1902:

> Our little Thérèse bestowed a great grace on me – it was more than two years ago, but the memory of it is still as clear as if it had happened yesterday. I was attending morning prayer, and my mind kept wandering – sadly, this is not rare. Suddenly, with the speed of lightning, something luminous appeared on my breviary. It was only afterwards that I fully realised that what I had seen was a hand. I immediately said to myself: 'It is my little Thérèse, calling me to order.' So many times, since then, I have wished I could see that beautiful hand again; but I never have. I assure you it was not my imagination; it was real.[7]

When she was finally established in the Visitation order at Caen, Léonie fully embraced their life with its ideal of gentleness, joy, humility and simplicity. Acutely aware of her limitations, and sincerely humble, she still believed she had "just enough wit" to become a saint. Moreover, following the self-acceptance of The Little Way she no longer worried about her imperfections and limitations: 'I know that Jesus asks for nothing of His lowly one but effort; and so I am far from being discouraged, for I want to remain in my complete helplessness, which is my strength.'[8] She followed so well the instructions of Thérèse to accept her imperfections, and to go to Jesus through trust and love, that she was even able to laugh about her own deficiencies. Among her visitors was Violette Castel, the sister of Marie of the Trinity, one of Thérèse's novices and a close friend of the saint. Madame Castel once exclaimed: 'I spent such lovely moments with Sister Françoise-Thérèse during our visits! She might be described as good sense united with the love of God. She is a real saint – and so humble! She makes everyone love her!'[9] Léonie was fully conscious of how far she had come through the grace of God: 'My childhood was dreadful, disfiguring our beautiful and holy family. How merciful God has been to me!'[10] She proved her gratitude and love by her self-surrender to the will of God as taught to her by Thérèse: 'I

---

7. *Ibid.*, pp. 91-92.
8. *Ibid.*, p. 91.
9. *Ibid.*, p. 88.
10. *Ibid.*, p. 91.

could not be more self-abandoned. I believe I have reached the point where God wishes me to be, for I love what he does above all else; I do not want to choose anything else.'[11]

On July 11, 1937, Léonie hung on every word of the radio transmission of the blessing of the magnificent new basilica at Lisieux dedicated to her sister Thérèse. One might well wonder how the seventy-four-year-old religious felt when, in a sermon given by the Bishop of Lisieux, her other sisters Pauline, Marie and Céline, all Carmelites like Thérèse, were mentioned by name, but of herself not a word. It was an unfortunate omission, but Léonie was no stranger at being overlooked or cast in second place. Moreover, the person whose tears fell to the floor with joy, as she knelt listening to Cardinal Pacelli, the future Pope Pius XII, honouring her sister Thérèse was no longer the 'Poor Léonie' of old. She was quite a different proposition altogether. The turbulence of her difficult life had undergone an amazing transformation. Indeed, there came a time when she became the centre of attention herself for the best of reasons. The Visitation convent at Caen began to receive visitors who wanted to meet Léonie. On one occasion she was even asked to sit beside the papal legate, Cardinal Vico. Far from finding such attention appealing, Léonie wanted to remain in obscurity. Her desire to remain hidden is reflected in the amusing story of the priest who expressed a wish to meet the sister of St Thérèse. The portress at the reception told him she thought it would be impossible. Moreover, she added that he would not be missing anything: 'It isn't worth the trouble.'[12] It was only when he later expressed his amazement to the chaplain at the sister of St Thérèse being spoken about in such a manner that he found out he had been tricked by Léonie herself.

When Léonie lay dying from a stroke she could not speak and had to thank the nuns who had come to show their affection with sign language. She smiled when one of her companions recited lines from one of Thérèse's most beautiful poems *Why I Love You, Mary*:

You came to smile on me in the morning of my life,
Come smile on me again, Mother, for evening is near.[13]

11. *Ibid.*, p. 91.
12. Baudouin-Croix, *ibid.*, p. 111.
13. *Ibid.*, p. 115. See also *Collected Poems of St Thérèse of Lisieux*, trans. A. Bancroft, Leominster: Gracewing, 2001. p. 229.

Her Prioress, Mother Marie-Agnes Debon, tearfully blessed Léonie and embraced her on behalf of her remaining sisters, Pauline and Céline.

After news broke of Léonie's death on June 12, 1941, visitors from across the world began to descend on the Visitation convent in Caen to honour the sister of the famous St Thérèse–but as a saint in her own right! Despite the burden of a difficult life, she had followed Thérèse on her Little Way and allowed the grace of God to transform her into the saint she wanted to be. Since her demise Léonie has also become an intercessor with petitions and expressions of thanks for graces received arriving at the Visitation convent in Caen from throughout the world. They include letters from anguished parents with difficult children. Sometimes they are written to express gratitude for graces or to claim miraculous cures have been wrought through the intervention of Léonie. The inspiring story of Léonie Martin is a profound reminder of the transforming power of The Little Way of St Thérèse of Lisieux, with its bold confidence in the merciful love of God and self-acceptance, not least for those who are dealt a difficult hand in life.

Chapter Four

The Humility of Céline Martin: Living The Little Way

It seemed like too much happiness to hope for. Very often, as she sat on the balcony of the Lisieux monastery, on summer evenings during the hour of silence before matins, Thérèse would say to herself: 'Ah! if only my Céline were here near me!' But this desire was not merely about fondness for her sister: '…it was for her soul, so that she might follow my Little Way.'[1]

'Echo of My Soul'

Céline Martin would later become Sr Geneviève of the Holy Face. Of the saint's four surviving sisters, she was the closest to Thérèse in both age and affection. Thérèse once described her as the 'sweet echo of my soul.'[2] Their souls were, indeed, intimately bound together. As a child, Thérèse followed Céline around everywhere and was known within the family as 'Céline's little girl'—Thérèse being four years her junior. Later, a spiritual bond developed between them when Céline became the confidante of Thérèse's thoughts in early 1887. That summer, the year before Thérèse entered Carmel, they shared remarkable ecstatic conversations in the 'belvedere,' a little summer room on the top floor of the family home. Céline generously delayed her own Carmelite vocation, so as to facilitate Thérèse's entry at the age of fifteen and to care for their father in his final illness.

For Céline, this trying time was also one of spiritual growth. When she visited Thérèse at the Carmel, their conversations were reminiscent of those in the 'belvedere.' The spiritual bonding between the two had by no means diminished. But it had changed

---

1. Stéphane-Joseph Piat, *Céline – Sister Geneviève of the Holy Face: Sister and Witness of Saint Thérèse of the Child Jesus*, San Francisco: Ignatius Press, 1997. p. 67.

2. *Ibid.*, p. 13.

in character. Their relationship was no longer one between equals. On March 1st, 1889, when Thérèse had been in Carmel less than a year, Céline had already written to her in the language of a disciple: 'I always come *after* you; I am another you, but you are the reality while I am only your shadow.' Thérèse records: 'Since my entrance into Carmel, I can say that my affection for Céline was a mother's love rather than a sister's.'[3] Their spiritual association reached new heights when Thérèse invited Céline to join her in her now famous 'Act of Oblation to Merciful Love.' Céline recalls: 'O Jesus, you accepted us as little Victims of your Merciful Love. I am the first one to have followed her Little Way. She opened the door, and I dashed in after her...'[4]

Arrival of an 'Other Self'

Céline entered the Carmel of Lisieux on September 14th, 1894 at the age of twenty-five. By that time Thérèse, already spiritually mature, was effectively the novice mistress. She rejoiced at the arrival of the sister whom she thought of as her 'other self': 'when I saw her enter here – and not only enter, but given to me completely to instruct – when I saw how God exceeded my desires, I understood the immensity of his love for me.'[5]

By now, Céline was an independent and talented woman who had refused several proposals of marriage. She was well read and an able artist. She had taken to the new invention of photography; it was she who made Thérèse one of the most photographed saints in history. Above all, she brought a small notebook of Old Testament texts into the Carmel that was instrumental in Thérèse's discovery of her Little Way. Céline was an excellent organiser and tireless worker, despite her frail health; she suffered from stomach trouble and frequent toothaches. Her numerous gifts were always in demand. She wrote several works, including a memoir of her sister and short biographies of her saintly–now 'Venerable'–parents, Louis and Zélie Martin.

The Fiery Carmelite

On entering Carmel, Céline instantly knew she had made the

3. *Story of a Soul*, Washington, DC: ICS Publications, 1996, p. 176.
4. Piat, p. 107.
5. *Ibid.*, p. 67.

right decision. She experienced a deep peace. However, she still found the monastery routine difficult. Adapting to community life among people from varying backgrounds and temperaments was particularly difficult for one so autonomous, headstrong and opinionated. Her fiery temperament gave way to many an outburst, which she would immediately regret bitterly.

The process of detachment and self-renunciation was also painful for her. And the fact that Thérèse was her novice mistress won her no favours. Although she was at heart an open and generous disciple, Céline still tended to be self-centred. She was deeply devout, yet retained a certain vestige of worldliness: 'I really had been steeped in [the world] too long not to be affected by it,'[6] she said. Thérèse formed her elder sister with the same wisdom and firmness as she did the other novices. At times, it was a difficult process for them both. On one occasion, Thérèse was even humiliated by Céline.

Mercy Stoops Down

The scourge of Jansenism, the seventeenth-century heresy, with its severe image of God and excessive fear of eternal punishment, still left its mark on France two centuries later. Within the Lisieux Carmel there were nuns who generously, but mistakenly, offered themselves to divine justice on behalf of sinners. Thérèse, in contrast, through her own deep insights, came to see that the love of God was synonymous with divine mercy: 'He is compassionate and filled with gentleness, slow to punish, and abundant in mercy, for He knows our frailty, He remembers we are only dust. As a father has tenderness for his children, so the Lord has compassion on us!!'[7]

Thérèse saw that the mercy of God stoops down to help those who realise their powerlessness and seek help with confidence. She held the omission of such trust to be actually offensive to God. The need for confidence in divine mercy was, therefore, a constant requisite of Thérèse in the formation of her novices. Céline was told: 'if we place all our confidence in the good God, and constantly put forth our best efforts, while hoping everything from His Mercy, we too shall receive the reward of the greatest saints.'[8]

6. Piat, p. 73.
7. *Letters of St. Therese of Lisieux* 226; cf. Ps 102:8, 14, 13.
8. Sr Geneviève of the Holy Face, *A Memoir of My Sister St Thérèse*, Gill: Dublin

Embracing The Little Way

The well-intentioned Céline, despite her best efforts, found the going difficult in her formation. She felt she was making little or no progress. She said to Thérèse: 'It seems that the more I desire to advance in virtue, the worse I become. I long to become sweet and patient, humble and charitable, but I do not think I shall ever succeed…'[9] She was so discouraged at times that she thought of giving up. But Thérèse patiently helped her sister to persist.

Thérèse made it clear to Céline that she must always expect to fall, but that like St Paul she should accept her human frailty and look upon it in a positive light.[10] Céline eventually came to see the wisdom in her sister's spiritual teaching: 'She made me find my joy in believing that I was a "very little soul" whom God constantly had to support because it was nothing but weakness and imperfection.'[11] It was this humility, or remaining little before God, that gave rise to The Little Way. From the time Céline first embraced her sister's 'little doctrine', humility became the virtue that attracted her most. She practised it with great courage.

From Delusion to Acceptance

Getting Céline to accept herself as she was required all of Thérèse's considerable skills as a spiritual guide. Any illusion the novice had of being self-sufficient in the pursuit of sanctity was exposed. Thérèse knew just how difficult self-acceptance can be. She had an acute understanding of why we should have a radical mistrust of ourselves: we have a frightening capacity for self-delusion because of our self-love. Seeing ourselves as we are requires immense humility. As novice mistress, Thérèse was unsparing in her efforts to root out the pride of her charges. Céline, for example, was given to stressing her victories and excusing her failures. Thérèse exposed this deception:

> You must never believe, when you don't practise virtue, that
> it is due to some natural cause like illness, time, or grief…
> What is necessary for you now is not to practise heroic virtues
> but to acquire humility. For that, your victories must of ne-

and P.J. Kenedy: New York, 1959, p. 211.

9. Sr Geneviève of the Holy Face, *A Memoir of My Sister St Thérèse*, Gill: Dublin and P.J. Kenedy: New York, 1959, p. 22.

10. cf. 2 Cor 12: 9-10

11. Piat, p. 77.

cessity always be mixed with failures, so that you cannot take any pleasure in thinking about them.[12]

Céline learnt to resist the temptation to deny, or alter, the facts of a difficulty she was facing. Thérèse also taught her to surrender her imperfections to the mercy of God without delay. This rapid self-surrender, in humble confidence, avoids all the pitfalls of immediate self-scrutiny or any attempt to confront a problem on our own. Equally, it puts an end to self-pity, brooding or, worse still, despair. When, in later years, Céline was well established in The Little Way, she explained: 'far from despairing over [our sins] or from giving in to a proud and disagreeable impatience because of them, we use them rather to deepen our distrust of self. We then go on to a greater confidence in God's merciful love which forgives completely, raises us up at once, and overwhelms us with His favours and with His love.'[13]

Giver and Gift

Thérèse taught her charges that sanctity has nothing to do with the acquisition of merits. In other words, our salvation cannot be bought, no matter how heroic we may consider our deeds to be. On the contrary, it is free–God being both the giver and the gift of our holiness. This does not, of course, mean that we are to make light of our sins. And it does not put an end to the need for works. Thérèse knew that authentic love for God is proved by its being expressed in action. The saint spelt out for Céline the paradoxical relationship between trust and works:

> We must do everything in our power, give without counting the cost, practise virtue at every opportunity, deny ourselves constantly, prove our love by all kinds of attentions and marks of affection, in a word, do all the good deeds in our power for the love of God. But since all that is really very little, it is important to place all our trust in him who alone sanctifies all deeds, and can sanctify without them…Yes, when we have done all that we think we should do, we must admit that we are worthless servants…but hope nevertheless that God will give us, free, all that we desire. That is what The Little Way of childhood is all about.[14]

12. *Ibid.*, pp. 74-5.
13. Sr Geneviève of the Holy Face, p. 22.
14. C. O'Mahony, ed and trans., *St Thérèse of Lisieux by Those Who Knew Her*,

Passive and Active

Part of the genius of Thérèse was that she saw that the smallest acts of virtue done through love have infinite value. They became an important element in proving her love for Jesus. But the greatest proof of her love was self-abandonment. Self-surrender in the manner of Thérèse means that we humbly and confidently embrace God's will in advance, in every detail and circumstance of our life, whether happy or sad. And because the abandonment of Thérèse is focused on each passing moment, there is no lamenting the past or worrying about the future. Incorrectly understood, abandonment gave rise to the discredited movement of Quietism in the sixteenth and seventeenth centuries. With its emphasis on passivity, it dispensed with the need for works; in some versions, it disregarded ethics altogether.

Thérèse was acutely aware of the danger of being branded a Quietist if her spiritual doctrine were badly explained. So she went out of her way to explain that The Little Way does not put an end to active effort on our spiritual journey. When giving evidence at the tribunal investigating the cause of Thérèse, Céline testified: 'She explained to me then with great vehemence that if the authentic spirit of childhood was based on surrender to and trust in God, it was based no less on humility and sacrifice.'[15] While Céline courageously followed her sister's teaching and increased her efforts to correct her faults, so as to please the Lord, she was also made well aware that these works had value only through the merits of Christ.

A Flame in the Sky

Céline cared for Thérèse during her illness with great tenderness and had the privilege of receiving a smile from the saint moments before she died: 'as I placed a small piece of ice on Thérèse's parched lips, I received in return a beautiful smile... Her superhuman expression was full of encouragement and promise as though she were saying to me: "Go on with courage, my Céline; I shall be with you."'[16] The saint was not long dead before she began to fulfil her promise. When Céline fled from the infirmary with grief, that last evening in September, 1897, she went outside to the cloister,

---

Dublin: Veritas Publications, 1995, p. 137.

15. *Ibid.*, p. 137.
16. Sr Geneviève of the Holy Face, p. 240.

naively hoping to catch a glimpse of Thérèse in the heavens. But it was raining. Then a strange thing happened. As she leaned against one of the columns, sobbing, she wished that the stars would come out. Immediately, she found herself looking at a star-studded sky. Her uncle and aunt, returning home from the Carmel at that very moment, were also struck by the sudden change of weather.

Nine days later, Céline saw 'a kind of flame coming from the depths of the sky' when she was making the way of the cross in the cloister: 'At the same moment,' she reported later, 'I felt something supernatural and exclaimed: "It's Thérèse!" The interior grace I received then is beyond my powers of expression; it was one of the greatest graces I have ever received. In a flash, I had the answers to difficulties that had depressed me for a long time. All my groundless worries disappeared; Thérèse's Little Way of trust, surrender, humility, and childlikeness was explained to me and I understood it fully.'[17]

'Rocket' to Heaven

Céline carried out her mission on behalf of her sister with a formidable determination. She was warned by an official at the process for the beatification, for example, that if there were any mention of 'a special Way,' her sister's cause would be 'infallibly doomed.'[18] Céline stood her ground. And her determination was vindicated. When, on August 14th, 1921, Benedict XV officially elevated her sister's teaching, Céline recalls: 'my joy reached heights never again attained, not even on those other memorable days later when my little sister Thérèse was first beatified and then canonized by Holy Mother Church.'[19] She also asserted that her sister's doctrine was no longer merely a 'way' because: 'by its swift and direct current we are raised like a rocket to the very Heart of God Himself.'[20]

Céline, an endearing and inspiring witness to Thérèse's liberating spiritual doctrine, died on February 25th, 1959. She survived her famous sister by over sixty years. In that time, she grew in holiness by following The Little Way of love and confidence. She continued to have human imperfections. But there was one vital difference.

17. O'Mahony, p. 166.
18. Sr Geneviève of the Holy Face, p. 39.
19. *Ibid.*, p. 39; cf. Piat, pp. 111-2.
20. Sr Geneviève of the Holy Face, p. 106.

While Céline worked hard to correct her faults, she was no longer discouraged by her failures. She learned from Thérèse how to
see her weaknesses in a positive light and to trust confidently in
Merciful Love. And she left us with a most inspiring testimony to
the effectiveness of her beloved sister's Little Way:

> On what would I base my confidence? Ah! I know well what
> it is; it will be on my miseries, on my defects, on my faults
> themselves. It will be in procession with them that I present
> myself before God, full of assurance, because then his pity
> will be my portion. He will save me, not because of my good
> works, but because of his goodness.[21]

---

21. Piat, p. 162.

II
Spiritual Teachings of Saint Thérèse

Chapter Five

Taking the Lift: The Little Way of St Thérèse

Many of us are faced with a choice between the stairs or the lift on a daily basis. In her quest for holiness, St Thérèse of Lisieux famously compared her own spiritual efforts with such a choice. As a young Carmelite nun, who entered religious life at fifteen by special dispensation, she set about becoming a saint by trying to take heaven by storm. But she failed.

Less than Perfect

We should always aspire to perfection, but sometimes we torment ourselves in our attempts to reach heaven. Somehow we believe that our Creator will settle for nothing less than the best. When we discover, as we do in so many different ways, that we are less than perfect, our grand plan for sanctity often implodes.

It is a predicament that arises out of an unrealistic view of ourselves. But even more seriously, it is rooted in a false idea of God. We should take heart, however, from the fact that Thérèse found herself in a somewhat similar cul-de-sac when her initial valiant efforts to become holy failed.

Never one to throw in the towel, the indefatigable young religious from Normandy came to the logical conclusion that there had to be another approach. She had, after all, a desire to become a saint. And she knew from reading St John of the Cross that God would never allow desires that could not be fulfilled.

Yet she was not measuring up to the great saints like Paul, Augustine and Teresa of Avila. So, she had to take stock.

An Elevator for Little Souls

Thérèse eventually concluded there was a place in heaven for little souls as well as the great ones: "I understood that our Lord's love is revealed as perfectly in the most simple soul who resists his grace in nothing, as in the most excellent soul."[1] It was then a matter of finding another route to sanctity: "one that was very straight, very short and totally new."[2]

By way of illustration she seized upon what was then a recent invention, the lift: the elevator "I wanted to find an elevator which would raise me to Jesus, for I am too small to climb the rough stairway of perfection." Thérèse searched the scripture for the elevator.

In two biblical passages she found what she was seeking: "Whoever is a little one, let him come to me!"[3] and "As a mother caresses her babe, so I will comfort you. I will hold you at my breasts, and will rock you on my knees."[4]

The Lift to Holiness

Thérèse found the "lift" for which she was searching: "The elevator which must raise me to heaven is your arms, O Jesus!"[5] But there was one condition. Rather than growing up, she was to remain little. She was to accept her powerlessness, and have boundless trust in the divine mercy.

Nothing, not even her imperfections, was to discourage her any more. "God remembers we are only dust," she said.[6] "As a father has compassion for his children, so the Lord has compassion on us!"[7] She would later say to one of her novices, "What offends him and what wounds his heart is the lack of confidence."[8]

---

1. St Thérèse of Lisieux, *Story of a Soul*, Washington, DC: ICS Publications, 1996, p. 14.

2. *Story of a Soul*, p. 207.

3. Proverbs 9: 4.

4. Isaiah 66: 12-13.

5. *Story of a Soul*, p. 208.

6. *Letters of St Thérèse of Lisieux*, trans. John Clarke, Washington, DC: ICS Publications, 1988, vol. 2, p. 1093.

7. *Ibid.*

8. *Letters of St Thérèse of Lisieux*, trans. John Clarke, Washington, DC: ICS Publications, 1982, vol. 1, 568.

The Little Way

The Little Way of St Thérèse is centred on the infinite mercy of God, and recognises that everything is a grace. Since it believes that Providence is in control from moment to moment, it means proactively embracing the will of God in every detail and circumstance of our life.

Once established in her new doctrine, Thérèse observed, "Jesus is doing all in me, and I am doing nothing."[9] She was no longer trying to save herself, stumbling on the "stairs." Now she was in the "lift," being rapidly made holy by the grace of God.

Because everything is a grace, Thérèse came to realise that God has no need of our works. But The Little Way is not an invitation to do nothing.

She also knew that, paradoxically, we prove our love by works. But she was also aware that works without love count for nothing. Within the walls of the then little-known Carmelite convent in Lisieux, she would become the greatest saint of modern times by her self-surrender to "Merciful Love," and by "not allowing one little sacrifice to escape, not one look, one word, profiting by all the smallest things and doing them through love."[10]

Confidence and Gospel Living

The "little doctrine" of St Thérèse is new, in that it represents the basic gospel truth of salvation in a fresh and ingenious way. I sometimes like to think of it as the great parable of the Prodigal Son writ large. For it was the deep insights of Thérèse into the divine love, that gave rise to her so-called Little Way of spiritual childhood. Thérèse came to equate God's love with the mercy of God. Thus, she sometimes referred to it as "Merciful Love." And her insights gave rise to an audacious confidence in the mercy of God.

Like St Paul, Thérèse's doctrine teaches us how to look upon our imperfections in a positive way. It encourages us to accept ourselves as we are, and even to rejoice in our weakness.

Thérèsian hope is actually based on an awareness of our spiritual poverty. Of course, that does not mean we are to make light of our

---

9. *Letters*, vol. 2, p. 796.
10. *Story of a Soul*, p. 196.

sins. On the contrary, we must see our faults and failings for what they are. And once they are clearly identified we must acknowledge our guilt before God.

We must repent and do our best not to repeat them. But equally The Little Way insists that we are not to brood, despair or become impatient over them. We can certainly learn to distrust ourselves because of them, and to be more aware of our tendency for self-seeking. But the secret is to surrender ourselves to the mercy of God with total confidence–and without delay!

Confidence

Confidence is pivotal in The Little Way. It is the key to unlocking the transforming power of God's great mercy. It guarantees a loving response from our merciful and self-effacing Creator who, so touchingly, is always waiting to stoop down and share the divine life with us, if we but ask.

Abandonment

Confidence has a close companion called abandonment. Indeed, Thérèse sometimes uses the words interchangeably. Once established in the humility and confidence of The Little Way we gradually learn how to approach life with an attitude of self-surrender to the will of God.

The gospel incident about Jesus' "true kinsmen" was one of Thérèse's favourites.[11] In her beautiful poem, *Why I Love You, Mary*, Thérèse anticipated the Second Vatican Council when she refers to Our Lady as her Son's first disciple:

> 'Who is my brother, who my sister, mother?
> He is that, who does my will'
> Jesus the Saviour said.[12]

Each Moment Counts

Thérèsian abandonment means embracing in advance whatever one is confronted with in life–happy or sad–in each passing mo-

---

11. Mk 3: 31-15.

12. See *Poems of St Thérèse of Lisieux*, trans. A. Bancroft, London: Fount 1996, p. 176.

ment. There is no lamenting the past or worrying about the future. It is the true measure of our confidence and the ultimate proof of our love for God. Nowhere is it more poignantly expressed, than in Jesus' prayer in Gethsemane: 'let your will be done, not mine.'[13] Clearly, it is not always easy, but once inside the "lift," all things are possible.

---

13. Lk 22: 42.

Chapter Six

The Abandonment of Saint Thérèse

In 1889 St Thérèse of Lisieux thought she had a clear idea of what counts as perfection: "Sanctity does not consist in saying beautiful things, it does not even consist in thinking them or feeling them; it consists in suffering and suffering everything."[1] Four years later she revised her definition of holiness to "Perfection consists in doing His will."[2] This important shift in her thinking meant she would never again ask for suffering. She was, however, still prepared to suffer joyfully but only if it were the will of God. Despite the fact that abandonment now took primacy over suffering in her spirituality the latter reached an intensity in her life that leaves us deeply moved. Indeed, it is more accurate to say martyrdom became her lot. On the day she died her self-surrender was tested to its endurance. Her lungs ravaged by tuberculosis, Thérèse was suffocating to death without the help of medication. The young Carmelite cried out to God for pity and to the Blessed Virgin Mary for help. The prioress, Mother Marie de Gonzague, attempted to comfort the dying nun by telling her the agony would shortly be over. Thérèse was not convinced. The Prioress then asked the dying twenty-four-year-old a searching question: "And if this were the will of God to leave you for a long time on the cross, would you accept it?" Sister Marie of the Trinity, her novice and friend, reports that Thérèse replied positively with an intonation of extraordinary heroism.[3] Thérèse's head then fell back on the pillow with a calmness and resignation that made it difficult for those present to

---

1. *Letters of St Thérèse of Lisieux.* Washington, DC: ICS Publications, 1982, pp. 557-558.
2. *Ibid.*, p. 795.
3. See P. Descouvemont, *Thérèse of Lisieux and Marie of the Trinity.* New York: Alba House, 1997, pp. 38-40.

hold back their tears. It was all too much for Marie of the Trinity who then left the room. This poignant scene in her dying hours shows that Thérèse's revised understanding of holiness in terms of abandonment endured to the very end.

Although the language of abandonment only became dominant late in the life of St Thérèse it is present to a lesser degree at an earlier stage. There is no doubt for example, that Thérèse practised abandonment when she met opposition to her early entrance into Carmel in 1887. The self-surrender of that period, however, is characterised more by activity as compared to its mature expression a decade later when it becomes a deeply ingrained and all-embracing state in her spiritual life. It was not until 1893 that abandonment begins to assume a central place in her spirituality. The theme looms large in her correspondence that summer with her closest sister Céline. On July 6 abandon is mentioned for the first time in one of her letters: "....my director, who is Jesus, teaches me not to count up my acts. He teaches me to do all through love, to refuse Him nothing, to be content when He gives me a chance of proving to Him that I love him. But this is done in peace, in abandonment, it is Jesus who is doing all in me, and I am doing nothing."[4] At this stage Thérèse made a crucial discovery that changed her approach to becoming a saint. She saw the gospel truth that everything is a grace. She now understood that love alone is sufficient, and God has no need of our works. Our salvation, in other words, does not rest on giving but in receiving. It is free. God does all. Her new approach to holiness marked a fundamental move away from a 'slide-rule' spirituality based on the stock piling of merits.

In a letter to Céline in that autumn the commitment of the young religious to self-surrender as the ultimate proof of her love for God gathers momentum. She proposes St Cecilia as a model for Céline. Although Cecilia is the patron saint of music, Thérèse liked to refer to her as "the saint of abandonment." This is because when caught between her commitment to virginity, and her unavoidable betrothal to a heathen, St Cecilia courageously abandoned herself to the unwelcome situation as a manifestation of the will of God. On April 28, 1894, Thérèse wrote a poem *The Melody of Saint Cecilia* for Céline's birthday because "I would need a tongue other than that of this earth to express the beauty of a soul's abandon-

---

4. *Letters* p. 796.

ment into the hands of Jesus."[5] We can hear that heavenly voice in another of her fifty poems *Surrender's the Delicious Fruit of Love*[6] which she wrote a few months before she died. The third stanza is particularly evocative:

> And from its branches fair
> (The tree is Love) there came
> A fruit that's sweet and rare
> Surrender is its name.

Merciful Love

The distinctive shape of Theresian abandonment does not emerge, however, until late 1894/early 1895 with her new appreciation of the divine mercy. Indeed, the particular practice of abandonment by Thérèse from that time was in direct proportion to her understanding of the self-effacing nature of God's love and her own powerlessness. Once in possession of this insight the remaining few years of her life become a living canticle to what she calls Merciful Love. At the end of 1894 Thérèse took stock of her spiritual life. She compared her own efforts to become a saint with the great saints like St Augustine, St Teresa of Avila and St Paul with whom, ironically, she would have so much in common. She had unsuccessfully tried to storm heaven through sheer self-will. Still she felt she had so many imperfections like falling asleep at prayer. She could easily have become discouraged but for two reasons. First, the resolution she made at her First Communion never to do so, and secondly, St John of the Cross had taught her that God can never inspire desires that cannot be fulfilled. There was only one logical conclusion for Thérèse. She had to persist with her quest for holiness as she was. And with haste. After all, what if she died young with nothing to show for her life? She found her answer in the variety of nature: "Just as the sun shines simultaneously on the tall cedars and on each little flower as though it were alone on the earth, so Our Lord is occupied particularly with each soul as though there were no others like it."[7] Thus, if the little ones

---

5. *Letters*, p. 850.

6. See *Poems of St Thérèse of Lisieux*, trans. A. Bancroft, London: Fount, 1996, pp. 166-169.

7. St Thérèse of Lisieux, *Story of a Soul*, trans. J. Clarke, Washington, DC: ICS Publications, 1996, p. 14.

outwardly appear to be less favoured it is not because they are less perfect. Their beauty rests in being themselves: "I understood, too, that Our Lord's love is revealed as perfectly in the most simple soul who resists His grace in nothing as in the most excellent soul."[8] No matter how great or small the soul, then, perfection consists in being what God wills us to be. Thérèse, of course, numbered herself among the little ones. She knew that the smaller she became the more Merciful Love would intervene in her life. After further reflection and prayer, she wondered whether there was a rapid route to Heaven. She urgently needed a means to sanctity that was very straight, very short and totally new; a Little Way like the one Franciscan Father Alexis Prou spoke about at his inspiring retreat from October 8-15,1891. About his preaching on abandonment and mercy she said: "He launched me full sail on the waves of confidence and love."[9] But at that time she was afraid to make the leap because of the prevailing climate within the convent. Indeed, she was even forbidden by Mother Marie de Gonzague to speak to the preacher again. Now ready for this saving spiritual adventure, however, she seized on the metaphor of a recent invention, the elevator, for her direct route to heaven.

Humility and Confidence

Providentially it was Céline (Sr Geneviève of the Holy Face) who provided the breakthrough. When she joined the local Carmel on September 14, 1894, she brought with her some notebooks comprising a small anthology of Old Testament passages. Thérèse found her Little Way as a result of pondering these texts. The first passage was Proverbs 9:4: "Whoever is a little one, let him come to me!" made her feel God was addressing her about God's self and her own sanctification. She believed she was that little one. The second text was Isaiah 66: 12-13: "As one whom a mother caresses, so I will comfort you, you shall be carried at the breasts, and upon the knees they shall caress you." She had found the shortcut to Heaven for which she was looking: "Ah! Never did words more tender and more melodious come to give joy to my soul. The elevator which must raise me to Heaven is Your Arms,

---

8. *Story of a Soul*, p. 14.
9. *Ibid.*, p. 174.

O Jesus!"[10] But there is one condition. Rather than growing up she was to remain little. All her expectations had been surpassed. Those who come to God with blind confidence, having humbly accepted their powerlessness, become beneficiaries of God's merciful love. From now on Jesus would carry her to the destination that she could not find on her own accord. During 1895 when she began the first manuscript of her diary she confirmed that the words of Psalm 23 had been realised in her: "The Lord is my shepherd, I shall want for nothing."

The condescending mercy of God and her own spiritual poverty ingrained itself deeply in the soul of St Thérèse. This gave rise to a boundless confidence in the divine mercy that in turn spilled over into an unqualified abandonment. Now everything is confidently surrendered to Merciful Love. Not least her imperfections. She would continue to do her best but her shortcomings were no longer allowed to discourage her. In a striking image Conrad De Meester sees confidence as the bridge across the abyss that separates humility from Merciful Love. This idea is not to be understood as a neat linear development. The construction of the bridge is ongoing in the spiritual journey.[11] There is no doubt that when Thérèse frequently listened to her novices lamenting their shortcomings she not only insisted that confidence in Merciful Love was not only a wise attitude but she held its omission to be actually offensive to God: "....what offends Him and what wounds His Heart is the lack of confidence." Indeed, even if she had on her conscience all the sins that could be committed her confidence would not have been diminished. Handing over the reins to God certainly did not mean the end of suffering but it did give her peace and the certitude that she had found the way to holiness.

Attracting the Love of God

Under the influence of a residual Jansenism, it was the prevailing custom in the Lisieux Carmel for the nuns to heroically offer themselves as victims to God's justice for the sins of the Third Republic. But God's justice held no such fears for Thérèse who had already understood God's love in terms of mercy. On the morning of June 9, the Feast of the Holy Trinity, Thérèse was thinking of

10. *Story of a Soul*, p. 208.
11. *Letters*, p. 568.

such generous souls but was not drawn to their approach. She saw that her courageous sisters were tackling the wrong problem. The justice of God was not the real issue. It was deeper than that. The real problem is that the divine love so gentle and self-effacing is rejected by so many who seek happiness in the idols of materialism and empty pleasures. Although the merciful love of God is infinite we have it within our discretion because of our free will to close off its flow. This is not only a catastrophe for those who cut themselves off from God though sin but it is also a tragedy for God because it prevents the divine love from intervening in their redemption. Seeing that God's love could be turned back upon itself by ungrateful sinners St. Thérése also saw that it needs to be requited. With a stroke of genius she saw the solution. She and others could reverse this tragic state of affairs by accepting the divine love others so blindly refuse On June 11th, Thérèse and Céline knelt before the statue associated with Thérèse's miraculous cure, the Virgin of the Smile. Thérèse recited her Oblation to Merciful Love for them both. Now we have entered the period of Theresian abandonment proper. This momentous event in the history of spirituality represents the climax of her self-surrender centred as it now was on the condescending mercy of God. As Bishop Guy Gaucher puts it: "This act of oblation followed the interior movement which had prompted the discovery of the way of confidence. It was merely the symbolic expression of it. Fire had replaced the lift, the 'holocaust' being the total sacrifice of the victim consumed by the fire of love."[12]

Spiritual Childhood

It is one thing to discuss Spiritual Childhood but putting it into practice is quite another. Such was the conviction of Thérèse that she possessed a spiritual treasure she taught it with absolute self-assurance. Her doctrine, indeed, became central to her role as novice mistress. And the spiritual child was frequently used as the image of the abandoned soul. Céline said "she wanted us to be like little children who possess nothing as their own and who depend entirely on their parents for their needs. She urges us to live only from day to day without laying by any spiritual store for the

---

12. G. Gaucher, *Story of a Life*, San Francisco: Harper, 1993, p. 147.

future."[13] When Sister Marie of the Trinity expressed her need for more strength and energy to practice virtue Thérèse replied: "And if God wants you to be weak and powerless like a little child, do you think you will be less worthy? Love your powerlessness, your soul will draw more profit than if, supported by grace, you achieve with a certain flair heroic act which fill your soul with personal satisfaction and selfish pride."[14]

Although it is commonplace in Theresian literature and numerous Popes have on various occasions recommended image of the spiritual child is one that can easily be misunderstood. While it can serve as a doorway into the heart of the teaching of Thérèse it also ironically, has the potential to distort the very doctrine it attempts to describe. An immediate danger in this imagery is that The Little Way of spiritual childhood might be seen as childish. We can well imagine this danger being especially present when we hear Thérèse herself speak in terms that are open to misunderstanding such as: "One can be happy to feel weak and miserable."[15] The reality of course could not be more different. Thérèse had put aside all childish behaviour since the time of her 'Christmas conversion' on Christmas Eve in 1886. Furthermore, as seen at the outset The Little Way effectively calls for self-immolation and is not for the fainthearted. Even a cursory look at Thérèse's own life, not least her last agony, can verify her spiritual doctrine is not a charter for mediocrity. Her sister Céline (Sister Geneviève of the Holy Face) when giving evidence at the tribunal investigating the cause of Thérèse testified: "She explained to me.... with great vehemence [my italics] that if the authentic spirit of childhood was based on surrender to and trust in God, it was based no less on humility and sacrifice..."[16] André Combes also raises another problem with the imagery of spiritual childhood. He draws our attention to the fact that it is all very well for those of us who find it easy to think of ourselves as a child of God. He wonders about those souls for whom God is remote and dreadful? For them the images of the Fatherhood of God and the spiritual child might not be readily

---

13. Sr Geneviève of the Holy Face, *A Memoir of My Sister St Thérèse*, Dublin: Gill and New York: P.J. Kennedy, 1959, p. 32.

14. *Thérèse of Lisieux and Marie of the Trinity*, p. 79.

15. *Ibid.*, p. 79.

16. C. O'Mahony, ed and trans, *St Thérèse of Lisieux by Those Who Knew Her*, Dublin: Veritas Publications, 1995, p. 137.

entertained. But what if such souls were convinced that this God was not unapproachable, stern, and remote as the imagery might indicate "...but is Love which takes the initiative to stoop down, regardless of our virtue, to share his own nature and life? Is it not the case that I, regardless of who I am, can become a child by grace of the God more loving than a mother?"[17] It is precisely because Thérèse had this experience that she saw it as her mission to share with others her Little Way. We must begin to grasp the meaning of Spiritual Childhood not as an abstract notion but as it was understood by the saint herself. As l'Abbé Combes says: "... it is only by giving ourselves, as Thérèse did, to that Love which stoops to us, in abandonment of itself, that each of us will know what it is to be a humble and trusting child of such love – the child of God himself."[18]

The Movement of Abandonment

In what he calls the movement of abandonment, Victor de la Vièrge spells out the implications of self-surrender to the will of God in our daily lives.[19] The movement of abandonment is seen to have three stages: "Clearly seeing reality, accepting it, offering it." First, if we have a problem, we must see it for what it is. Therefore any temptation to deny or alter the facts must be resisted. If we become discouraged by some fault we must not deny our imperfection by projecting the blame elsewhere. Neither should we brood about our weakness. Theresian abandonment requires that we humbly acknowledge our faults and plead guilty in the confidence of obtaining mercy from God. As a result, Thérèse never tired of obliging her novices to see them-selves as they are. Establishing an objective understanding of the situation that confronts us requires a constant awareness of this potential shortfall because of our self-love. Once seen for what it is the proper disposition to our weakness goes beyond mere acceptance in Theresian abandonment. Indeed, it is the failure of souls to grasp this insight that blocks their progress. Once our weakness is seen for what it is and accepted positively in the light of Merciful Love, we must avoid

17. A. Combes, *Saint Thérèse and Her Mission*. New York: P.J. Kennedy & Sons, 1955, p. 55.

18. *Ibid.*

19. See V. de la Vièrge, *Spiritual Realism of St Thérèse of Lisieux*, Milwaukee: The Bruce Publishing Company, 1961.

anytemptation to introspective self-pity. Having patiently accepted one's failings the third step calls for an immediate self-offering. We must avoid immediate self-scrutiny, or worse despair, and rapidly abandon ourselves to God's mercy by handing over our imperfections. Deep reflection only arises at a later stage.

Blind Trust

Surrender *à la* St Thérèse means that we believe that divine Providence is in control from moment to moment. Believing then that the hand of Christ Jesus is guiding everything we must enthusiastically embrace God's will in every detail and circumstance of our life–be it happy or sad. There is no picking or choosing. And because the surrender of St Thérèse is focused on the present moment there is no lamenting the past or worrying about the future. This level of Theresian abandonment reminds us of Jean-Pierre de Caussade's teaching on the complete abandonment to Divine Providence. He too believed that such a degree of abandonment in the duty of the present moment is only sustained through confidence in God's unchangeable love. Arguably, however, the strongest influence on Thérèse, if only unconsciously, may have been her patron St François de Sales. His approach to abandonment is certainly helpful in illuminating Theresian abandonment.

In his writings St. François makes a distinction between three degrees of abandonment. Resignation, the first, is a mere acceptance of what cannot otherwise be changed. One accepts death willingly, for example, but would still prefer to live. This effort of submission is inferior to what he calls holy indifference that lacks effort. Unlike resignation, which submits to the will of God with effort, because it has no other choice holy indifference responds to events and circumstances without effort. It operates out of a peaceful attitude of living the presence of God's will.

Higher still, however, is what he calls "a simple waiting on God's will" which anticipates and accepts in advance what has not yet been revealed. He allowed no exceptions to this rule: "It is not sufficient to accept God's will generally. We must accept it in every detail and circumstance. Not only must we be prepared to be ill, if that is God's will, but we must be prepared to accept the particular kind of illness, in the time and place, and with those people, which He shall choose for us."[20] It is then a matter of "As thou wilt and how thou wilt."

The Danger of Quietism

Thérèse was acutely aware of the danger that she could be branded as a Quietist if her doctrine was badly explained. Incorrectly understood abandonment gave rise to the discredited movement of Quietism in the 16th and 17th centuries where a complete passivity dispensed with works and, in one version, even disregarded ethics altogether. She fully appreciated the paradox that although God has no need of our works, our love for God does require an expression in action if it is authentic. The Little Way does not, therefore, put an end to effort on our spiritual journey. Indeed, the practice of virtue is an essential element in The Little Way. We should also note, in a related sense, that Vatican II cautions against using abandonment as an excuse for avoiding action in addressing human needs. It would be wrong, for example, to expect the victims of social injustice to bear their pain in the here-and-now in the expectancy that a provident God will make up for it in the hereafter. We should be clear, therefore, that self-abandonment does not mean the servile submergence of one's own will in the will of God in a quietistic sense. It is more an "exchange of wills," one that requires explanation in terms of the Trinity."[21]

Although one remains subject to the will of God, it is done by choice in the knowledge that self-reliance in the pursuit of sanctity does not work. St Thérèse reflects this principle when she boldly states that "the good God will have to carry out my will in heaven, because I have never done my own will on earth." [22]

Abandonment and Confidence

Theresian abandonment really cannot be discussed in isolation from the other dominant aspects of her spirituality. I suggest that it is helpful to think in terms of an organic relationship embracing

20. J. P. Camus, *The Spirit of St François de Sales Longmans*. London: Green & Co., 1953, p. 143.

21. H. U. von Balthasar, *Two Sisters in the Spirit*. San Francisco: Ignatius Press, 1992, p. 320.

22. *Last Conversations*. Washington, DC: ICS Publications, 1977, p. 91.

the three elements: *Humility, Confidence* and *Abandonment,* and that these interdependent aspects developed in intensity relative to the Saint's ever deepening insights into the divine love. This process eventually resulted in the discovery of her spiritual doctrine, The Little Way. This threefold schema is consistent, for example, with what St Thérèse told her sister Pauline (Mother Agnes of Jesus) about her new teaching two months before she died:

"Mother, it's the way of spiritual childhood, it's the way of confidence and total abandon..."[23] But what are we to make of the famous passage of St Thérèse in a letter dated September 17, 1896, to her sister Marie (Sister Marie of the Sacred Heart): "It is confidence and nothing else but confidence that must lead us to love?" Does this contradict everything that has been said so far? Well, we could note for a start that only a few days earlier Thérèse told Marie in a letter that "Jesus is pleased to show me the only road which leads to this divine furnace, and this road is the abandonment [Thérèse's italics] of the little child who sleeps without fear in his Father's arms..." Upon closer examination there is, in fact, no contradiction. Therefore, there is no need to remove self-surrender as the ultimate proof of St Thérèse's love for God. As Conrad De Meester points out, St Thérèse seems to often use confidence and abandonment as synonyms. He cites her letter of September 17 as an example where confidence is preferred to abandonment in order to emphasise the dynamic nature of her attitude for her hesitant sister Marie. Moreover, he finds in general that the confidence of Thérèse is difficult to distinguish from her abandonment.[24]

Finally, St Thérèse had a deep and balanced devotion to the Blessed Virgin Mary as her spiritual Mother. Although she was well aware of Our Lady's privileges, she was also convinced that Our Lady's life was very simple and that Mary lived by faith just like anyone else. This is nowhere more evident than in the 'true kinsmen' gospel story (Mk 3, Matt 11, Lk 8), which was a favourite of hers. Significantly, the idea that Mary was the first of her son's disciples is captured in terms of abandonment in the twentieth

---

23. *Ibid.,* p. 257.
24. See C. De Meester, *The Power of Confidence.* New York: Alba House, 1998, pp. 305-307.

stanza of her poem *Why I Love You, Mary!*:

> Who is my brother, who my sister, mother?
> He is that, who does my will
> Jesus the Saviour said.

Chapter Seven

Saint Thérèse: Suffering and the Will of God

Zélie Martin and four other people in the room could find no signs of life in her three-month-old daughter Thérèse, including the nurse, on whose knee she "lay like one dead." Zélie was concerned that she was going to lose her ninth-born child to enteritis after four of her children had already died, three of them in infancy. Zélie then thanked God that her baby had died so peacefully. However, after a quarter of an hour, Thérèse opened her eyes and smiled. She was completely cured. Zélie's plea for St Joseph's intercession had been answered after all.

For the next few years, Thérèse grew-up to be a happy and agreeable child: "Oh! everything truly smiled on me on this earth…" However, her happy disposition changed with the death of her mother on 28 August 1877, at forty-four years of age. As a result, Thérèse, then four-and-a-half, was afflicted with a severe hypersensitivity that lasted for nine-and-a-half years, accompanied by a succession of other sufferings. When her sister and 'second mother' Pauline entered Carmel on 2 October 1882, Thérèse fell apart: "I shed bitter tears because I did not yet understand the joy of sacrifice. I was weak…" The pain of separation gave rise to a strange nervous condition on Easter Sunday, 25 March 1883. Thérèse, now ten, was brought to death's door once again with "convulsive tremblings, hallucinations and incoherent ramblings." She was suddenly cured of the baffling attack when the Blessed Virgin Mary appeared to her on 13 April 1883. But she then suffered a spiritual trial when doubts were raised in her mind about the apparition after being inundated with questions about it. Thérèse's uncertainty was not erased until the veracity of what she saw was confirmed when she prayed at the basilica of Our Lady of Victories in Paris. Frightened by a retreat given by Abbé Louis-Victor Domin for her Second

Communion, from 17-21 May 1884, she got an horrendous attack of scruples. The loneliness arising out of her closest sister and confidante Céline leaving her school in 1886, continuing scruples and intermittent headaches gradually combined to undermine Thérèse's health again. Her father Louis decided to take Thérèse out of school at thirteen, on 3 April 1886, and brought her to a private tutor Mme Papinau instead. The painful wounds of separation were opened-up all over again when her eldest sister and godmother Marie also became a Carmelite nun on 15 October 1886. Thérèse was healed of scruples, at the end of the month after turning to her four little brothers and sisters in heaven with a simple, heartfelt prayer. Two months later, Thérèse's childhood sufferings would come to an end with her "Christmas conversion."

When the family returned home from midnight Mass in 1886, her tired father Louis was disappointed to find that Thérèse, then fourteen, was still clinging to the childhood custom of examining the presents after they were left in her shoes in the chimney corner. On her way upstairs to remove her hat, Thérèse overheard her annoyed father say: "Well, fortunately, this will be the last year!" Louis' words pierced Thérèse's heart as she ascended the stairs to remove her hat. Céline advised her not to go back downstairs for fear it would cause her too much grief. But suddenly, in a miraculous instant, Thérèse's hypersensitivity was completely cured. She then cheerfully dashed down the stairs and joyfully opened her gifts as normal in front of her delighted father. Her strength of mind had been suddenly restored: "…the gentle little child of only one hour, changed the night of my soul into rays of light."

Thérèse was only two years into her childhood sufferings when she felt within her heart a great desire to suffer on the day after she made her First Communion, 9 May 1884: "Suffering became my attraction; it had charms about it which ravished me without understanding them very well. Up until this time, I had suffered without loving suffering, but since this day I felt a real love for it…" Her embrace of suffering in the midst of so much pain becomes comprehensible when we understand that, although suffering is a consequence of sin, as François Jamart explains, "…In God's wisdom… it has been transformed into a means of sanctification, a proof of love, an instrument for the salvation of souls." When Thérèse entered the local Carmelite monastery in Lisieux on 9

April 1888, at fifteen, the rigours of the enclosed life were exactly as she expected: "...suffering opened wide its arms to me and I threw myself into them with love." Shortly before her profession, she declared she had come to Carmel to save souls and to pray for priests. But a great suffering visited her from without when her father's mental problems began: he went missing on 23 June 1888 and eventually entered a mental hospital on 12 February 1889. A year later Thérése identifies suffering with holiness in letter dated 26 April 1889 to Céline (LT 89): "Sanctity...consists in suffering and suffering everything." However, four years later she changed her mind.

In the summer of 1893, Thérése arrived at the conclusion that there is an even greater means of proving our love for God than suffering: abandonment (or surrender) to the will of God. She redefines her new understanding of holiness in a letter to Céline dated July 6:[1] "...Perfection consists in doing His will..." Thérèse also mentions the word abandon in the same letter for the first time: "...my director, who is Jesus... teaches me to do all through love, to refuse Him nothing, to be content when He gives me a chance of proving to Him that I love Him. But this is done in peace, in abandonment..." Thérèse's newfound priority of pleasing God by doing his will is further evident when she proposes St Cecilia as a model of self-surrender in a poem for Céline The Melody of St Cecilia for Céline. She did so because, as she wrote on 26 April 1894,[2] "I would need a tongue other than that of this earth to express the beauty of a soul's abandonment into the hands of Jesus." Thérèse's unconditional self-surrender would take some time before it reached a deeply rooted and all-embracing state.

During her early years as a Carmelite nun, Thérèse suffered great anguish from an extreme dread of sin. She tried to take heaven by storm to cope with her fear, but failed. But then she was launched full sail on a "sea of confidence of love" after a liberating retreat by the stand-in retreat master, the Franciscan Père Alexis Prou, from 8-15 October 1891. Thérèse's self-abandonment began to quicken at the end of 1894-early 1895 when she discovered her Little Way, with its newfound confidence in the merciful love of God and self-acceptance of her flawed human nature. She not only

1. *Letters of St Thérèse of Lisieux*. Washington, DC: ICS Publications, 1982, p. 142.
2. *Ibid.*, p. 161.

began to accept her imperfections but, like St Paul, even to rejoice in them. Remarkably, Thérèse barely mentioned mercy before the end of 1894: "The bulk of her writings... (some 350 pages of letters, poems and plays) feature the noun 'mercy' only once, and the adjective 'merciful' also just once." But in the first paragraph of *Story of a Soul*, dated January 1895, she began to sing only one song, as she would eternally: "The Mercies of the Lord."

Thérèse's self-surrender developed in direct proportion to the development of her newfound audacious confidence in God's gratuitous merciful love and an increasing humble awareness of her own powerlessness: "Oh Jesus! Why can't I tell all little souls how unspeakable is Your condescension? I feel that if You found a soul weaker and littler than mine, which is impossible, You would be pleased to grant it still greater favours, provided it abandoned itself with total confidence to Your infinite mercy." By the time she offers her Act of Oblation to Merciful Love six months later, a symbolic expression of her Little Way, she "understands God's merciful love 'better than ever,' and abandons herself to it more effectively until this abandonment becomes second nature." By the end of 1895, as she was finishing the first of the three autobiographical manuscripts of the *Story of a Soul*, her self-abandonment had reached its maturity: "...I possessed suffering and believed I had touched the shores of heaven...Now, abandonment alone guides me. I have no other compass!" Although Thérèse revised her definition of holiness, she would still embrace suffering as the will of God if it came her way, but crucially—she would no longer ask for it.

Self-surrender in the manner of St Thérèse is based on her confidence that God is guiding everything in each passing moment. Accordingly, she would enthusiastically embrace the divine will in every detail and circumstance of her life–be it happy or sad: "Everything is a grace!" Because her self-abandonment was focussed on the present moment there is no lamenting the past or worrying about the future. Thérèse also fully appreciated the paradox that although God has no need of our works, our love for God does need an expression in action to be authentic.

Thérèse's final two-fold sufferings began during the Easter weekend of 1896. However, despite their excruciating intensity, she exhibited an inspiring underlying peace that nothing could disturb because of her state of abandonment to the will of God.

The first sign of pulmonary tuberculosis became evident on the night of Good Friday, April 3. Two days later, on Easter Sunday, her bewildering Trial of Faith began and prompted her to sit in solidarity at the table of unbelievers. Her test lasted to the end of her earthly life.

Thérèse was literally suffocating to death on the day she died, 30 September 1897, when the then prioress Mother Marie de Gonzague confirmed that she was in her last agony and about to die: "Yes, my poor child, but perhaps God wills to prolong it for several hours." Thérèse then replied in a spirit of heroic self-surrender that moved those present in the infirmary to tears: "Well, all right!...I would not want to die a shorter length of time."

Chapter Eight

Saint Thérèse and the Holy Face: the Glory of Being Unknown

To Hide in the Desert

It is a wonderful irony that St Thérèse should have become one of the most famous names in the world. Photographs taken by her sister Céline (Sr Geneviève) in the Lisieux Carmel have made Thérèse one of the most photographed saints in history. And she has been revered in so many ways, across the globe, with cathedrals, basilicas, shrines and churches built under her patronage. She was named a 'Secondary Patron' of France, making her an equal of her heroine Joan of Arc. She was also named 'Patron of the Missions' alongside St Francis-Xavier. More recently, she was elevated to the rank of Doctor of the Church. Thérèse has also made an impact across the denominations. Her relics, for example, were recently received at York Minster. Together with Francis of Assisi, she is the only other saint from the west to be venerated by Russian Christians after the schism. Her universal influence has also touched Moslems; there is a shrine at Shoubra, offered by the Moslems of Cairo to the 'little saint of Allah.'

Such widespread recognition could not, however, have been further from the thoughts of the young girl from Normandy, who at the astonishing age of two had wished to become a religious[1] and who, by the age of nine, had said that she 'would like to be a hermit and go away...in a faraway desert place'[2]–deciding that the local Carmel was 'the desert where God wanted me to go...to

1. St Thérèse of Lisieux, *Story of a Soul*, Washington DC: ICS Publications, 1996, p. 20.
2. *Ibid.*, p. 57.

hide myself.'[3] Furthermore, she was under no illusions as to the austere life that lay in store for her in the enclosed life at the Lisieux Carmel. The enduring peace she experienced after this decision was confirmation that it coincided with God's will.

'I Longed to be Forgotten'

When Thérèse entered that monastery at the age of only fifteen, she rejoiced at being given the religious name, 'Thérèse of the Child Jesus.' The Child Jesus remained an important part of her identity and spirituality until the end. But on the day she received the habit, her desire to be hidden from the world took a new turn. She chose to complete her religious name with the title, 'and of the Holy Face.' After entering the convent, the Holy Face had become central to her piety, and her devotion intensified at the time of the mental illness of her father, Louis Martin, which revealed itself soon after she entered Carmel. Curiously, Thérèse had had a mysterious vision, when looking out of an attic window one day around the age of six or seven, while her father was away on a business trip to Alençon: she saw a man in the garden, dressed exactly like her father only much more stooped, and a cloth was hiding his face. It was only when Thérèse was in Carmel, and going over this 'strange scene' with her sister Marie, that they both suddenly realised its significance. It had been a prophetic vision of their father's illness, and Thérèse saw at once the link with the Holy Face of Jesus:

> Just as the adorable Face of Jesus was veiled during His Passion, so the face of His faithful servant had to be veiled in the days of his sufferings in order that it might shine in the heavenly Fatherland near its Lord, the Eternal Word![4]

The year before she died, Thérèse recalled how her sister Pauline (now Mother Agnes of Jesus) had been responsible for deepening her devotion to the Holy Face:

> Until my coming to Carmel, I had never fathomed the depths of the treasures hidden in the Holy Face. It was through you, dear Mother, that I learned to know these treasures. Just as formerly you had preceded us into Carmel, so also you were first to enter deeply into the mysteries of love hidden in the

---

3. *Ibid.*, p. 58.
4. *Ibid.*, p. 47.

Face of our Spouse. You called me and I understood. I understood what real glory was. He whose Kingdom is not of this world showed me that true wisdom consists in 'desiring to be unknown and counted as nothing,' in 'placing one's joy in the contempt of self.' Ah! I desired that, like the Face of Jesus, 'my face be truly hidden, that no one on earth would know me.' I thirsted after suffering and I longed to be forgotten.[5]

'The Foundation of All My Piety'

Some years previously, at Pauline's suggestion, their father, by then a widower, enrolled himself and his other four daughters in the Confraternity of the Holy Face. On April 26, 1885, Thérèse was registered as entry 'No. 7382' in the name of 'Mlle Martin Thérèse.' The modern devotion has its origins in the veneration of the veil of St Veronica with its imprint of the Holy Face. The Holy Face was venerated as early as 610, and popular devotion continued in varying degrees in later centuries. A notable revival in France took place in 1845 after a revelation to a nun at the Carmel of Tours, Sr Marie of St Peter. The Lord told her that he would imprint his features on the souls of all who would venerate his Holy Face in reparation for blasphemy and other outrages. The devotion was further promoted by Léon Dupont, later known as 'the holy man of Tours,' and now declared Venerable. He kept a lamp burning every night before a picture of the Holy Face at his home. Many came to pray there, including the sick, and to be anointed with oil from the lamp. It later became a public place of veneration. The Confraternity is still run from this very house at 8, rue Bernard-Palissy, Tours.

Devotion to the Holy Face was introduced into the Lisieux Carmel in 1847. When Thérèse contemplated the downcast eyes of the Holy Face on Veronica's veil, in the picture which the Carmel had been able to obtain, she was drawn to the Suffering Servant readings from Isaiah.[6] She said to Pauline: 'These words of Isaias… "There is no beauty in him, no comeliness, etc.," have made the whole foundation of my devotion to the Holy Face, or, to express it better, the foundation of all my piety. I, too, have desired to be without beauty, alone in treading the winepress, unknown to

---

5. *Ibid.*, p. 152.
6. Isaiah 52:13–53:12.

everyone.'[7]

So pivotal had the devotion become in Thérèse's spirituality that on her deathbed the picture of the Holy Face was brought from the convent chapel to the infirmary for her to venerate it. Her devotion was reflected in a number of other ways, too: she made the feast of the Holy Face her own; several of her prayers between 1896 and the beginning of 1897 are centred on contemplation of the Holy Face; she painted the image on vestments and pictures; she carried a picture of the Holy Face on her heart; on her sickbed she pinned an image of the Holy Face from her breviary; her novices, including Céline, also added the Holy Face to their religious name; and the image is featured in most of her important poems—in particular, *My Heaven on Earth*[8] is her canticle to the Holy Face. And when Thérèse made her Act of Oblation to Merciful Love in 1895, she asked God to look upon her 'only in the Face of Jesus and in His heart burning with Love.'[9]

'How She is Unknown Here!'

Thérèse desired to be unknown by everyone, even those among whom she lived. Apart from a few nuns, she had largely succeeded in hiding her inner life within the community. Incredibly, she even managed to conceal the extent of her sanctity from Pauline. When Thérèse gave her sister the first eight chapters of the autobiographical recollections she had written under obedience, Pauline left the manuscript aside for all of three months. When she finally got around to reading it, she was astonished at how little she knew her own sister:

I did not take the time to read it until after the elections in the spring of that same year. Oh! then, how I regretted not having thanked her sooner, for she so much deserved this! my little Thérèse! But she, once her act of obedience was accomplished, was no longer concerned about it. This holy indifference touched me so much that I found the reading of her life all the more beautiful. I said to myself: And this blessed child, who wrote these heavenly pages, is still in our midst! I can speak to her, see her, touch her.

---

7. *Last Conversations*, p. 135.

8. *The Poetry of Saint Thérèse of Lisieux*, trans. D. Kinney, Washington DC: ICS Publications, 1995. 20.

9. *Story of a Soul*, p. 276.

Oh! how she is unknown here! And how I am going to appreciate her more now![10]

The Sand and the Roses

Thérèse used the image of a grain of sand to symbolise her desire to be hidden from the world. In a letter to her sister Marie (Sr Marie of the Sacred Heart), she wrote: 'Ask that your little daughter always remain a little grain of sand, truly unknown, truly hidden from all eyes, that Jesus alone may be able to see it, and that it may become smaller and smaller, that it may be reduced to nothing.'[11] This aspiration towards complete anonymity led to a new desire, the autumn before her death. Thérèse was hoping to go the Carmelite foundation in Hanoi, where she would be unknown to anyone. But it was not to be.

Thérèse contracted tuberculosis and died on September 30, 1897 at 7:20 in the evening. She was only twenty-four. Her burial in the local cemetery, on a hill outside the town of Lisieux, was a simple affair, with a handful of people in attendance. But before long, her anonymity would be at an end. Thérèse's heavenly mission on earth could begin: 'my mission of making God loved as I love Him, of giving my Little Way to souls.'[12] Ten days after Thérèse's death, Céline experienced an interior grace beyond words, after seeing 'a kind of flame coming from the depths of the sky.' She would later become the most determined champion of her sister's spiritual doctrine. The Little Way broke upon the world with the publication of *Story of a Soul*. Claims of apparitions, miracles and other favours soon abounded after Thérèse's 'shower of roses.'

---

10. *Last Conversations*, p. 18.
11. *Letters of St Thérèse of Lisieux*, trans. J. Clarke, Washington DC: ICS Publications, 1982, p. 49.
12. *Last Conversations*, p. 102.

Chapter Nine

Saint Thérèse: Her Greatest Devotion

When Sister Thérèse of the Child Jesus received her habit on January 10, 1889, she expanded her religious name. The sixteen-year-old Carmelite nun added: 'And of the Holy Face' to her signature in a note to a religious sister within the Lisieux convent. This was no mere passing whim brought on by the emotion of the special day. It amounted to a significant addition to her religious identity. fu if to underscore her full religious name, Thérèse is photographed, shortly before she died, with pictures of both the Child Jesus and the Holy Face.[1] Her devotion to the Holy Face, however, became dominant in her spirituality. Her closest sister Céline testified that '... we must recognize in the interests of objective truth, that her devotion to the Holy Face of Jesus transcended—or more accurately embraced—all the other attractions of her spiritual life.'[2] It must be emphasized, however, that the devotions of St Thérèse to the Child Jesus and the Holy Face are inseparable, and they both lasted to the end. As Guy Gaucher says: 'Far from being in opposition the Child Jesus and the Suffering Christ—they are deeply united. It is the one and the same person. From Childhood he knew suffering; naked on the straw of the cave, pursued by men, fleeing from Egypt...'[3]

The Holy Face at the Centre of Her Spirituality

The centrality of this devotion in the piety of St Thérèse is re-

1. On this topic see especially *The Prayers of St Thérèse*, trans A. Kane, Washington DC: ICS Publications, 1996, p. 105.

2. Sister Geneviève of the Holy Face, *My Sister Thérèse*, Rockford, Illinois: Tan Books, 1997, p.m.

3. G. Gaucher, *The Passion of Thérèse of Lisieux,* Homebush: St. Paul Communications, 1989, p. 227.

flected in the fact that when she made her profound *Oblation to Merciful Love* in 1895, her prayer begged that God would look upon her 'only in the Face of Jesus and in his Heart burning with love.' The special place of this devotion is evident in so many other ways. For example, the Holy Face in featured in most of her important poems; she dedicated a hymn to it; her prayers between 1896 and the beginning of 1897 are centred on contemplation to the Holy Face; she painted the image on vestments and pictures; she carried a small picture of the Holy Face on her heart; on her sick bed she pinned an image of the Holy Face from her breviary; her novices, including Céline, added the Holy Face to their religious name, and on her deathbed at the age of 24, she rejoiced when the picture of the Holy Face was brought from the chapel of the convent to the infirmary for her to venerate.

Thérèse's Discovery of the Devotion

It was another of her four sisters, Pauline (Mother Agnes), who deepened her understanding of this devotion. A year before she died, Thérèse recalls for Pauline: 'Until my coming to Carmel, I had never fathomed the depths of the treasures hidden in the Holy Face. It was through you, dear Mother that I learned to know these treasures. Just as formerly you had preceded us into Carmel, so also you were the first to enter deeply into the mysteries of love hidden in the Face of our Spouse. You called me and I understood. I understood what *real glory* was. He whose Kingdom is not of this world showed me that true wisdom consists in "desiring to be unknown and counted as nothing," in "placing one's joy in the contempt of self" Ah! I desired that, like the Face of Jesus, my face be truly hidden, that no one on earth would know me. I thirsted after suffering and I longed to be forgotten.'[4]

The Modern Devotion

The modern devotion has its origins in the veneration of the veil of St Veronica with its imprint of the Holy Face of Jesus. It was venerated in Rome as early as 610. Popular devotion to the Holy Face continued in later centuries in varying degrees. One notable time of revival took place in France in 1845 when it was revealed by Our

---

4. *The Story of a Soul*, trans. J. Clarke, Washington DC: ICS Publications, 1996, p. 153.

Lord to a nun in the Carmel at Tours, Sister Marie of Saint-Pierre (1816-1848), that he would imprint his features on the souls of all those who venerated his Holy Face in reparation for blasphemy and other outrages. The devotion was further promoted by Leon Dupont, later known as the holy man of Tours, and now declared Venerable. Many people came to his house in Tours where he kept a light burning before a picture of the Holy Face. The devotion was introduced into the Lisieux Carmel in 1847. The Confraternity of the Holy Face was established at Tours in 1848. On April 26, 1885, M. Martin enrolled himself and his five daughters in the Confraternity at the suggestion of Pauline, who had by that time entered the Lisieux Carmel. Thérèse is registered as entry No. 7382 in the name of 'Mlle Martin Thérèse.'

Thérèsian Devotion to the Holy Face

Conrad De Meester explains that the devotion of St Thérèse to the Holy Face had two aspects: ' ... .i) to love Jesus, whose suffering Face is for Thérèse the mirror of his love, and ii) to imitate Him in His profound humility.'[5] When Thérèse meditated on the Holy Face she used a picture of St Veronica's veil and the Suffering Servant of Yahweh readings from the prophet Isaiah (ch. 53:1-5 and ch 63: 1-5). On August 5, 1897, the month before she died, Thérèse told Pauline: 'These words of Isaiah: ' ... There is no beauty in him, no comeliness etc.,' made the entire foundation of my devotion to the Holy Face, or, to express it better, the foundation of all my piety. I, too, have desired to be without beauty, alone in treading the wine press, unknown to everyone.'[6]

The devotion of the young Carmelite to the Holy Face intensified at the time of her saintly father's mental illness. It would be difficult to exaggerate the pain and devastation his humiliation brought to Thérèse and her sisters. News of his affliction broke at the time Thérèse started her postulancy. Louis Martin went missing on June 23, 1888, and was found at the post office in Le Havre. He was placed in an asylum after wielding a gun in the imaginary defence of his children on February 12, 1889. The following July he was obliged to formally renounce the admin-

---

5. C. De Meester, *The Power of Confidence*. New York: Alba House, 1998, p. m.

6. *Her Last Conversations*, ed J. Clarke, Washington DC: ICS Publications, 1977, p. 135).

istration of his goods because it was feared his recklessness with money would leave him in danger of financial ruin. Referring to a vision she had of a man exactly like her father, with his head covered, in the Summer of 1879-1880, Thérèse asserts:

> It was indeed Papa, who was bearing on his venerable counte-
> nance and white hair the symbol of his glorious trial. Just
> as the adorable Face of Jesus was veiled during His Passion,
> so the face of His faithful servant had to be veiled in the
> days of his suffering in order that it might shine in the
> heavenly Fatherland near its Lord, the Eternal Word.[7]

On July 18, 1890, she again compares the humiliation of her father with that of the Passion of Jesus: 'Jesus has sent us the best chosen cross that He was able to find in His immense love... how can we complain when He himself was looked upon as a man struck by God and humbled! ...'[8]

Contemplating His Closed Eyes

In a letter dated April 4, 1889, to Céline, Thérèse wrote: 'Jesus is on fire with love for us... Look at His eyes lifeless and lowered!... Look at his wounds ... Look at Jesus in His face... There you will see How he loves us.'[9] It was indeed those downcast eyes that Thérèse contemplated in a wonderful two-way interplay of indirect communication with the Lord as she faced the Holy Face. The attraction of Thérèse to the devotion deepened with the commencement of her Trial of Faith in Easter 1896. In addition to having to endure the physical pain of her tuberculosis, she was beset by temptations to the faith for the entire duration of her illness. On August 6 in that same year, the feast of the Transfiguration, Thérèse solemnly consecrated herself to the Holy Face, together with her novices: Céline, her cousin Marie and Marie of the Trinity. Significantly, all four had already offered themselves to Merciful Love. In a conversation with Pauline, a month before she died, the dying Thérèse recalls, as she looked at the picture of the Holy Face: 'How well our Lord did to lower His eyes when he gave us His portrait! Since the eyes are the

---

7. *The Story of a Soul*, p. 47.

8. *Letters of St Thérèse of Lisieux*, trans. J. Clarke, Washington, DC: ICS Publications, 1982, p. 630.

9. *Letters*, p. 553.

mirror of the soul, if we had seen His soul, we would have died from joy. Oh, how much that Holy Face has done me in my life!'[10] Threse's poem, *My Heaven Here Below,* is her canticle to the Holy Face. The second last stanza links her tender devotion to the Holy Face with her entire mission to win souls for the Lord:

Your Face... ah, only that will be The wealth I ask as revenue: I'll hide in it, unceasingly; Then Jesus, I'll resemble You. Imprint in me those traits divine Your Gentleness of Face imparts; Holiness, then, will soon be mine - To You I'll be attracting hearts.[11]

10. *Last Conversations,* pp. 134-135.
11. *Collected Poems of St Thérèse of Lisieux,* trans A. Bancroft, Leominster: Gracewing, 2001, p. 91.

Chapter Ten

The Joyful Self-Acceptance of Saint Thérèse

During her early years in Carmel, Thérèse suffered great anguish from an extreme dread of sin. The malaise was easy to fester in a religious setting still feeling the weight of a residual Jansenism, the condemned 16th century teaching, with its bleak emphasis on sin and punishment. Even tiny failings were harshly judged by some. For example, Thérèse had been sternly reprimanded by the then chaplain for offending God when she confessed a difficulty with staying awake at Mass. However, during a retreat in September 1890, the Franciscan Alexis Prou enabled her to make considerable spiritual progress when he launched her "... full sail on the waves of confidence and trust."[1] But it was not until her self-acceptance a few years later that her troubled approach to sin really came to an end. Shortly before she died, Thérèse recalled how she had always felt little whenever she compared herself to the saints.[2] And how, taking courage from her belief that God cannot inspire unrealizable desires, she reasoned that despite her littleness she could still persist with her childhood desire for sanctity: "... so I must bear with myself such as I am with all my imperfections."[3] However, even that crucial decision would undergo further momentous development. In the same breath as her self-acceptance, Thérèse expressed a desire to find a route to sanctity equal to her littleness: "... a Little Way, a way that is very straight and very short and totally new."[4] Feeling too little to climb "the rough stairway of perfection" she searched in the Scriptures for some sign of an 'elevator,'

---

1. St Thérèse of Lisieux, *Story of a Soul*, edited by John Clarke O.C.D., Washington D.C: ICS Publications, 1996, p. 174.
2. See *ibid.*, pp. 207-208.
3. *Ibid.*, p. 207.
4. *Ibid.*

or 'lift,' to raise her to Jesus. She found the answer in her divinely inspired reading of two biblical extracts (Proverbs 9:4; Isaiah 66: 12-23) from the anthology her closest sister Céline (Sr Geneviève of the Holy Face) brought with her when she too entered the local Lisieux Carmel in September, 1894. The 'elevator' turned out to be nothing less than the arms of her beloved Jesus himself. She was overjoyed to discover her new Little Way and rejoiced to find that her initial self-acceptance was more than vindicated by God. Not only did she find there was no need to grow up but she now felt called to become more and more little—or humble—until she became absolutely little to the point of being forgotten. Jesus had surpassed all her expectations. No longer content with the mere acceptance of her imperfect self, she would, like St Paul, begin to actually rejoice over her innate weakness and make rapid advancement on her spiritual journey.

The idea of exulting over our human incapacity has, of course, nothing whatsoever to do with playing down the seriousness of sin. Indeed, Thérèse stresses the importance of taking responsibility for our faults; never to pass the blame elsewhere, and not to delay in expressing sorrow for our failings. Her closest sister and former novice Céline (Sr Geneviève of the Holy Face) summarizes well the nature of the relationship between self-acceptance and our powerlessness in The Little Way:

> We are not excusing or making light of sin by the mere fact
> that we recognize or even love our weakness and accept all its
> consequences. No, in this way, as a matter of fact, we become
> established in truth and we are saved from all self-delusion.
> Then from the very depths of our misery, which we then
> recognize better than ever, there springs up a cry of daring
> confidence in the infinite mercy.[5]

Without seeking to downplay sin in anyway, then, self-acceptance in the manner of St Thérèse teaches us how we can look upon our faults in a positive light. We start by looking upon our defects as a constant reminder of our innate weakness and complete dependence on God. She understood such an honest assessment of our human nature to be the truth and therefore pleasing to the Lord. Indeed, she expected to see new imperfections in her own life every

---

5. Sister Geneviève of the Holy Face (Céline Martin) *My Sister Saint Thérèse*, Rockford, Illinois: Tan Books, 1997, p. 21, footnote 17.

day. And she encourages us to be happy to see ever more clearly our own powerlessness. In other words, the more humble–or little–we are in patiently accepting ourselves just as we are the more it enables God's merciful love to intervene in our lives.

The spiritually liberating teaching of Thérèse unfolded against the background of her profound insights into the mercy of God. Conrad De Meester points out, Thérèse rarely mentioned the word 'mercy' prior to 1895: "The bulk of her writing...(some 350 pages of letters, poems, and plays) feature the noun 'mercy' only once, and the adjective 'merciful' also just once."[6] However, after her breakthrough she was full of the divine mercy, as is evident in the first paragraph of *Story of a Soul*: "...I am going to be only doing one thing: I shall begin to sing what I must sing eternally: "The mercies of the Lord.""[7] Thérèse also began to tenderly picture God as our merciful self-abasing creator who is always ready to stoop down to help his creatures, and share the divine life with them, when they were truly humble.

If humility–or 'littleness'–is the basis of The Little Way of Spiritual Childhood, the audacious confidence of Thérèse with its unlimited trust in the mercy of God is its unique feature.[8] As her profound insights into the divine mercy deepened at the time of her spiritual breakthrough her confidence became ever more breathtaking. She found that the more confidence she had in his mercy the more Jesus came into her life. Indeed, she is very clear that confidence is not only a wise attitude but that its omission is actually offensive to God. Moreover, she considers self-pity and other symptoms of brooding over our failings to be a major stumbling block to having such confidence. She blamed the source of such gloominess on a self-love that refuses to acknowledge the truth of our human incapacity. Adopting an attitude of confidence in the mercy of God is not always easy however. We have first to overcome any difficulties we may have with self-acceptance. Such was the case with the novices of Thérèse. Disheartened by their own imperfections they frequently sought her guidance. For example, Marie-Louise Castel (Sr Marie of the Trinity), the childlike trans-

---

6. Conrad De Meester, *With Empty Hands*, London: Burns & Oates, 2002, p. 64.
7. *Story of a Soul*, p. 13.
8. See Francois Jamart, O.C.D., *Complete Spiritual Doctrine of St Thérèse of Li-sieux*, New York: Alba House, Chapters 1-4.

feree from the Paris Carmel, expressed the wish for more strength and energy to practice virtue. Thérèse replied with a leading theme in her teaching on our incapacity:

> If God wants you to be weak and powerless as a child, do you think your merit will be any the less for that?... Resign yourself, then, to stumbling at every step, to falling, even, and to being weak in carrying your cross. Love your powerlessness; your soul will benefit more from it than if, aided by grace, you were to behave with enthusiastic heroism and fill your soul with self-satisfaction and pride.[9]

The self-acceptance of St Thérèse is not an invitation to do nothing. Indeed, she once cautioned Marie-Louise to be careful how she explained The Little Way lest it be mistaken as Quietism, the 17th century error that dispensed with works. Céline also reminds us: "Although her Little Way, the Way of Spiritual Childhood, is a way of blind and complete confidence, Thérèse was far from minimizing the role of personal co-operation...her own spiritual life was one long series of generous and consistent acts of virtue."[10]

When Marie-Louise shared her fear that God would be angry with her repeated faults, she received from Thérèse a consoling image of the comprehensive nature of the 'blind' merciful love of God:

> ...If the greatest sinner on earth repented of all his offenses at the last moment and died in an act of love, God would not stop to weigh up the numerous graces which the unfortunate man had wasted and the crimes he had been guilty of; he counts only that last prayer and receives him into the arms of his mercy without delay.[11]

Finally, Céline too found it very difficult to bear with her faults and even expressed doubt that she would ever succeed. Thérèse corrected her for not facing up to the truth of her weakness: "... let us humbly throw in our lot with the imperfect, and look upon ourselves as 'little souls' that God has to support every minute of

9. *St Thérèse of Lisieux by Those Who Knew Her*, edited by Christopher O'Mahony O.C.D., Dublin: Veritas, 1995, p. 250. See also Pierre Descouvment, translated by Alexandra Plattenberg-Serban, New York: Alba House, 2005, pp. 85-89.

10. Geneviève of the Holy Face, *A Memoir of my Sister*, p. 56.

11. Christopher O'Mahony, *Saint Thérèse of Lisieux By Those Who Knew Her*, p. 233.

the day."[12] A very talented but impatient woman Céline lived until she was almost 90. She eventually mastered self-acceptance and grew in holiness. While she worked hard to correct her failures, she no longer allowed them to discourage her. This is so touchingly evident in her eloquent testimony of what it means to be a humble and confident 'little soul.'

> On what would I base my confidence?... it will be on my miseries, on my defects, on my faults themselves. It will be in procession with them that I present myself to God, full of assurance, because then his pity will be my portion. He will save me, not because of my good works, but because of his goodness.[13]

---

12. *St Thérèse of Lisieux by Those Who Knew Her*, p. 151.
13. Stéphane-Joseph Piat O.F.M., *Céline*, San Francisco: Ignatius Press, 1997, p. 162.

Chapter Eleven

The Oblation to Merciful Love of Saint Thérèse

Twenty-two-year-old Thérèse was tearful, and quiet in herself, when she left the chapel after Mass on June 9, 1895. Her curious behaviour on that bright sunny morning, Trinity Sunday, attracted the attention of her closest sister and confidante Céline (Sister Geneviève of the Holy Face). Céline's interest grew when she unwittingly found herself in the middle of a drama as she was led along in tow by Thérèse, hurrying to catch up on Mother Agnes (Pauline, another of the four local Martin sisters within the Lisieux discalced Carmel). She witnessed a somewhat embarrassed Thérèse seek permission from Pauline to offer both herself and Céline as holocaust victims to the merciful love of God. Pauline did not fully understand the significance of the request at the time, but she granted permission anyway because she trusted Thérèse. When an elated Thérèse was alone again with an equally baffled Céline, her face lit up as she briefly explained that she would gather her thoughts and set about composing her now celebrated Act of Oblation to Merciful Love. Two days later, after requesting Pauline to have the wording of her self-offering checked by a theologian, Thérèse, with Céline kneeling by her side, recited the oblation for them both before the shrine of the miraculous Virgin of the Smile in the ante-room alongside the saint's cell. The act marked the summit of Thérèse's spiritual accent. Keeping the text in her book of the gospels next to her heart day and night, she recited the offering as often as possible.

Mass had just begun on June 9 when Thérèse suddenly had the unexpected inspiration that gave rise to her oblation: 'I received the grace more than ever before how much Jesus desires to be loved.'[1] Thérèse actually means here 'allowing Jesus to love us.'

1. *The Story of a Soul*, trans. J. Clarke, Washington DC: ICS Publications, 1996, p.

This unforeseen grace came about when she was thinking of those members of her own Carmel, who offered themselves to the justice of God in an attempt to deflect the punishment due to sinners by heroically bearing it themselves. At a time when Jansenism still lingered in France, which restricted the hope of salvation to a chosen few, some of the nuns were well-disposed to a book which taught incorrectly that such an offering represented one of the aims of the Carmelite Order.

Thérèse also had a zeal for souls, of course. It was after all the reason she entered Carmel. But she was far from drawn to the oblation to God's justice. Her newfound bold confidence in the divine mercy, the basis of her recently discovered spiritual doctrine, The Little Way, had already become the prism through which she contemplated and adored all the other divine perfections: '... even his Justice (and perhaps this even more so than the others)... What a sweet joy it is to think that God is Just, i.e., that he takes into account our weakness, that he is perfectly aware of our fragile nature...'[2]

Thérèse's deep insights into the mercy of God came to her after six years of trial and error since she became a Carmelite. She finally realized that salvation is a gift, and that her valiant but self-willed efforts to take heaven by storm had failed. Her point of departure on this new direct route to heaven was a humble acceptance of her flawed human nature while handing over the reins to the mercy of God with complete trust. The joyful experience of the tender, self-abasing infinite love then suffused her life with an intensity that left her with a single wish: to sing 'the Mercies of the Lord.'[3]

No wonder then Thérèse was grieved when she began to think about that very same self-abasing love of God being so widely rejected and turned back on itself She was deeply concerned, too, for those souls who so foolishly seek happiness in finite creatures that eventually disappoint. And by freely separating themselves from God they sadly prevent the divine mercy from intervening in their salvation.

But Thérèse was also hopeful that if she and others could console the rejected love of God by offering themselves as victims of

---

180.
 2. *Ibid.*, p. 180.
 3. *Ibid.*, p. 13.

holocaust to God's merciful love this calamity could be reversed, and the flow of those pent-up streams of divine tenderness would be released for the benefit of all souls. In this mode of reflection she spontaneously cried out from the depths of her heart during thanksgiving after Holy Communion:

> O my God! Will your justice alone find souls willing to im-
> molate themselves as victims? Does not your Merciful Love
> need them too? On every side this love is unknown, rejected;
> those upon whom you would lavish it turn to creatures,
> seeking happiness from them with their miserable affection;
> they do this in stead of throwing themselves in your arms
> and of accepting your infinite Love...If your Justice loves to
> release itself, how much more does your merciful Love desire
> to set souls on fire...O my God! Is your distained Love going
> to remain closed up within your Heart? It seems to me that
> if you were to find souls offering themselves as victims of
> holocaust to your Love, you would consume them rapidly...
> [and]that you would be happy not to hold back the waves
> of infinite tenderness within you. O my Jesus, let me be this
> happy victim; consume your holocaust with the fire of your
> Divine Love![4]

Thérèse's oblation is couched in the language of one of the biblical sacrifices. Called a 'holocaust' in Greek, it means 'wholly burnt' and originally intended the total immolation of a victim by fire. However, unlike the biblical sacrifice where the priest offered a non-human creature on behalf of a particular individual, Thérèse's oblation intends the complete spiritual self-offering of the person directly making the sacrifice. And she innovatively applied the traditional sacrificial terminology aptly to her own intentions. Céline explains how the old terms find new meaning in the Thérèsian context: 'The new state of the victim she proposed was martyrdom indeed, but a martyrdom of love.'[5] The word 'victim,' for example, signifies being 'overwhelmed' by a tidal wave of the tender love of God. And 'holocaust' points to being 'burned-up' by the divine love.

One can well imagine how traditional words like 'holocaust' and 'victim' might sometimes give rise to misunderstanding if taken out

---

4. *Ibid.*, pp. 180-181.
5. Sister Geneviève of the Holy Face, *My Sister Saint Therese*, Rockford, Illinois: Tan Books, 1997), p. 80.

of their Theresian context. The most obvious mistake is to assume incorrectly that the oblation to love necessarily entails suffering. A notable example is Thérèse's eldest sister and godmother Marie (Sr Marie of the Sacred Heart) who was scared to death when she was asked if she would like to become a 'holocaust victim' to the love of God. At first Marie declined the invitation on the grounds she had a dread of suffering and was moreover repelled by the very word 'victim.' However, her mind was put at rest when Thérèse reassured her that the oblation was not in fact a request for suffering. Marie went on to become one of the oblation's greatest advocates and was actually reciting it when she died.

A similar misinterpretation occurred in remarkable circumstances when the very Liturgical Office of Saint Thérèse itself had to be corrected in 1932, four years after it was first published. This amendment followed a complaint from Pauline who was alarmed that already in her own lifetime the thought of Thérèse had been so distorted. She could not rest until the wording 'inflamed with the desire for suffering' was altered to 'on fire with divine love.' Céline was no less adamant: 'The soul offering herself to love is not asking for suffering...'[6]

Any inclination to automatically link Thérèse's oblation with pain can be compounded if we come to it with the incorrect assumption that the attitude of the saint to suffering was consistent throughout her short life. While it is true, she once thought she had a clear idea of what counts as sanctity in terms of suffering for souls, she changed her definition of holiness to the doing of God's will in 1893. By the time of her death in 1897 her self-abandonment had matured to become a deeply ingrained and all-embracing state in her life. When she discovered her Little Way around late 1894, surrender to the divine will took priority over all her other desires as proof of her love for God. Thérèse observed the primacy of self-surrender by welcoming whatever life delivered in each pass-ing moment, be it happy or sad, confident that God is in charge from moment to moment.

Although doing the will of God eventually assumed primacy in her spiritual life, Thérèse continued to have a supernatural appre-ciation of the value of suffering. In keeping with the imperative of self-surrender in her new spiritual doctrine, which was now her

---

6. *Ibid.*, p. 84.

only happiness, she would still embrace suffering if it came her way, as indeed it did with an intensity that leaves us deeply moved, but, crucially, she would no longer ask for it.

While an attitude of self-abandonment became the primary means of proving her love for God, Thérèse also appreciated the paradox that although God has no need of our works our love still needs to be expressed in action. This she famously observed through her heroic practice of charity in small things.

A few days after making her self-offering to Merciful Love, which she presented to the Blessed Trinity through the hands of Our Lady, Thérèse received an answer from heaven. While beginning the Way of the Cross she was consumed by the Fire of Love. It was indeed as if she had been plunged into a furnace. Such was the intensity of the wound of Merciful Love she considered her life would have ended had it lasted a second later. Thérèse now felt that she would be better able to win souls for God. And she speaks of the oceans of graces that continued to inundate her soul since making the oblation. It is an experience she desired for all 'little souls', but the saint was also adamant that the recitation of the offering on its own is not enough and we must give ourselves entirely to God in a life of self-surrender to infinite love, the leading stance of her Little Way.

Chapter Twelve

The Prayer of Saint Thérèse

She was all of two-and-a-half years when she said her first prayer. When she was four she had notions of becoming an enclosed nun, along with her closest sister Céline. When told she would have to remain silent in the convent the child was puzzled. Raised in a devout home where vocal prayer was the rule, the idea of praying to Jesus without saying anything was beyond her. In the course of her short life things would change however. By the time she was twenty-four, a young Carmelite nun suffocating from tuberculosis, she had reached the heights of contemplation. Asked by Sister Geneviève of the Holy Face (Céline) what she said to Jesus when praying, during her sleepless nights of suffering, she replied: "I say nothing to Him; I love Him."[1]

It is said of St Thérèse that her life was a continual prayer. Even most of her poems are prayers. She herself confirms that she was always in the presence of God: "I do not believe I have ever been three minutes at a time without thinking of Him."[2] And it was not difficult for her to do so: "... we naturally think of the one we love."[3]

Praying really was simple for Thérèse:

> ... prayer is an aspiration of the heart, it is a simple glance directed to Heaven, it is a cry of gratitude and love in the midst of trial as well as joy; it is something great and supernatural

---

1. *Last Conversations*, ed. J. Clarke, Washington, DC: ICS Publications, 1977, p. 228.

2. Quoted by Guy Gaucher in *The Prayers of Saint Thérèse of Lisieux*, Introduction by G. Gaucher, O.C.D., trans. A. Kane, O.C.D., Washington, DC: ICS Publications, 1997, p. 22.

3. *Ibid.*

which expands my soul and unites me with Jesus.[4]

In her prayer she took the ordinary approach: 'I tell God what I want simply without any splendid turns of phrase, and somehow He always manages to hear me.' Neither did she seek extraordinary mystical experiences such as ecstasies, visions or revelations: 'I prefer the monotony of sacrifice.'[5] Similarly she preferred to contemplate Jesus, Mary and Joseph in their ordinary aspect, especially in the Gospels. Although Thérèse preferred free-flowing prayer she was still faithful to the two hours of daily prayer imposed by the Rule.

It is a comfort to recognize some familiar human traits in this great saint. She suffered dryness in prayer all her life. She often fell asleep while praying despite her best efforts to stay awake. But she was never distressed about this failing. She reasoned that God was responsible for the problem in the first place! It was a simple matter of doing our best in love, in the sure belief that God understands the sincere soul. Because Thérèse preferred to pray spontaneously rather than using formulated prayer, prayer books gave her a headache.

To her great mortification, Thérèse found the Rosary something of a chore! She found it difficult to meditate on the mysteries. But she still persisted. And she grew in confidence that Our Lady would be satisfied with her goodwill. While praying, it was love that mattered most for Thérèse. She understood that that is all God looks for in the midst of any distractions and dryness.

Thérèse, the contemplative emerges at an early age. She recalls that when accompanying her father while he was fishing, she was meditating without really knowing what it was. On her free afternoons from school she would retire to a private space and begin to think. She thought about God, life and eternity. Later she realised the nature of this new form of prayer:

"I understand now that I was making mental prayer without knowing it and that God was already instructing me in secret."[6] Thérèse also came to know the limitations of human language:

---

4. *Story of a Soul*, trans. J. Clarke, Washington, DC: ICS Publications, 1996, p. 242.

5. *Letters of St. Thérèse of Lisieux*, Washington, DC: ICS Publications, 1982, P. 620.

6. *Story of a Soul*, pp. 74-75.

"Frequently, only silence can express my prayer."[7]

Once Thérèse really became aware of the merciful nature of divine love she was full of it. This led to the discovery of her Little Way of humility, confidence and abandonment—her greatest legacy.

7. *Letters of St Thérèse of Lisieux*, trans. John Clarke, Washington, DC: ICS Publications, 1986, vol. 2, p. 764.

Chapter Thirteen

The '*olah* of St Thérèse: Consumed by the Fire of Love

Blazing a New Trail

The historic nature of the unfolding drama that began in the chapel of the Lisieux Carmel on June 9th, 1895, the feast of the Holy Trinity, was far from self-evident to some of its main actors. It started with a reflection of Thérèse while assisting at mass. She was thinking of those people, including members of her own Carmel, who offered themselves as victims to divine justice, in order to draw away the wrath of God from other sinners upon themselves. It was a heroic thing to do. But it was misguided. A residual Jansenism, with its emphasis on the severity of God's justice, still had an icy influence in Carmel. Thérèse did not warm to it. Such was her confidence in the mercy of God, the basis of her recently discovered Little Way, that she saw God's justice in a different light: 'even His Justice…seems to me clothed in love. What a sweet joy it is to think that God is Just, i.e., that He takes into account our weakness, that He is perfectly aware of our fragile nature. What should I fear then? Ah! must not the infinitely just God, who deigns to pardon the faults of the prodigal son with so much kindness, be just also toward me who "am with Him always"?'[1] It is no wonder, then, that this sacrifice found no attraction for Thérèse. As a result, she boldly prayed:

> O my God! Will Your Justice alone find souls willing to immolate themselves as victims? Does not Your Merciful Love need them too? On every side this love is unknown, rejected; those hearts upon whom You would lavish it turn to crea-

---

1. *The Story of a Soul,* trans. J. Clarke, Washington, DC: ICS Publications, Washington, 1996, p. 180.

tures, seeking happiness from them with their miserable affection; they do this instead of throwing themselves into Your arms and of accepting Your infinite Love… If Your Justice loves to release itself, this Justice which extends only over the earth, how much more does Your Merciful Love desire to set souls on fire since Your Mercy reaches to the heavens. O my Jesus, let me be this happy victim; consume Your holocaust with the fire of Your Divine Love![2]

When Thérèse hastened from the chapel that momentous bright morning, Céline (Sr Geneviève) was nonplussed as to her sister's excitement, but did what she was told and went along with whatever Thérèse had in mind. Another sister, Pauline (Mother Agnès), the then prioress, at first gave permission for Thérèse to make her oblation without attaching any importance to it. Little did either of them know that, as André Combes puts it, their twenty-two-year-old sister Thérèse was 'blazing a new trail of Christian spirituality.'

The Oblation and The Little Way

As with those people who made the offering to divine justice, Thérèse also would have understood her oblation in terms of one of the types of biblical sacrifice called, in Hebrew, the 'olah. The Greek translation is holocaust, meaning 'wholly burnt.' The idea behind this type of burnt sacrificial ritual is the total immolation of the victim, usually taken from sheep or cattle, so that its smoke or scent ascended to heaven where it was 'inhaled' by God. The 'olah of Thérèse was not identical with this Old Testament form: unlike the biblical ritual, where the priest offered a creature in the name of a particular individual, the 'olah of Thérèse involved the offering of the person directly making the sacrifice. She therefore invested the Old Testament sacrificial type with new meaning.

Any mention of becoming a holocaust victim to the mercy of God, let alone to divine justice, can be unintelligible and even somewhat terrifying to the modern mind. And not only in our own times. When Thérèse suggested the idea to her sister Marie (Sr Marie of the Sacred Heart), it frightened her to death! However, when Thérèse explained that it was not what it seemed, Marie's mind was put at rest. Céline would later explain the holocaust to merciful love in terms of abandonment to the will of God: 'The

---

2. *Ibid.*, pp. 180-1.

soul offering herself to love is not asking for suffering, but in yielding herself up entirely to the designs of love, she is accepting in advance all that divine Providence will be pleased to send her by way of joys, labours and trials.' It was effectively The Little Way of Thérèse in different guise. As Guy Gaucher explains: 'This act of oblation followed the interior movement which had prompted the discovery of the way of confidence. It was merely the symbolic expression of it. Fire has replaced the lift, the "holocaust" being the total sacrifice of the victim consumed by the fire of love.'

Reversing a Tragedy of Love

Crucial to understanding any sacrifice is the intention that lies behind it, and it is in the very intention behind the '*olah* of Thérèse that we catch sight of her genius. Her ritual is inspired by a particular grace: 'This year, June 9, the feast of the Holy Trinity, I received the grace to understand more than ever before how much Jesus desires to be loved.'[3] We should be aware, however, that Thérèse means something different here from what she appears to say at first sight. To love Jesus really means allowing him to love us. Thérèse had an acute realisation of the problem surrounding her new emphasis on the longing of God to be loved. Quite simply, the advances of God's love are widely rejected throughout the world. Rather than putting their trust in the one thing that can make them truly happy—infinite Love—so many people hand themselves over exclusively to finite creatures, at best a source of temporary happiness. This universal defection from the love of God is the scandal that Thérèse seeks to remedy in her 'Act of Oblation to Merciful Love.'[4] Thérèse could see that it was a tragedy for creatures as well as for the Creator.

The invitation of God is a call to self-transcendence, to become divinised in a created sense. Thérèse's '*olah*, then, is a means of bridging the gulf between God's loving invitation and the wholesale ingratitude of humankind. Thus, for Thérèse, the question of our redemption has less to do with satisfying the justice of God than with resolving the problem of the love of God being despised and turned back on itself. The self-offering of Thérèse seeks to reverse this tragic state of affairs. It is the means whereby the dam to the

3. *Ibid.*, p. 180.
4. *Ibid.*, pp. 276-7.

flow of God's love is released:

O my God! Is Your disdained Love going to remain closed up within Your Heart? It seems to me that if You were to find souls offering themselves as victims of holocaust to Your Love, You would consume them rapidly; it seems to me, too, that You would be happy not to hold back the waves of infinite tenderness within You.[5]

It was while she was making the Stations of the Cross a few days later that Thérèse received her answer: she experienced the fire of love. Such was its intensity that she considered her life would have been ended had it lasted one moment longer. As André Combes puts it so aptly: 'Now that the holocaust was accepted, fire from heaven consumed the victim.'

In *Story of a Soul*, Thérèse speaks of her new state of life and the 'oceans of graces' that inundated her soul after her oblation. Countless other people who have offered themselves to Merciful Love have had their lives similarly transformed. The profound importance of the '*olah* of Thérèse in relation to the love of God, and redemption of the world, cannot be overestimated.

---

5. *Ibid.*, pp. 180-1.

Chapter Fourteen

St Thérèse and the Child Jesus: Whispers from the Crib

Gifts from the Infant Jesus

When the fifteen-year-old Thérèse Martin was waiting to enter Carmel in her home town of Lisieux, she began to give some thought as to what religious name she might be given. Remarkably, she anticipated the very one that would be chosen for her: 'Thérèse of the Child Jesus.' This is how she would recall it in her autobiography:

> I wondered what name I would be given in Carmel. I knew there was a Sister Thérèse of Jesus; however, my beautiful name of Thérèse could not be taken away from me. All of a sudden, I thought of Little Jesus whom I loved so much, and I said: 'Oh! how happy I would be if they called me Thérèse of the Child Jesus!' I said nothing during the visit about the dream I had while wide awake. But to good Mother Marie de Gonzague, who was asking the Sisters what name I should be given, came the idea of calling me by the name I had dreamed about. My joy was great and this happy meeting of minds seemed to be a singular favour from my beloved Child Jesus.[1]

Before entering the convent, Thérèse already had a special reason to be devoted to the divine Child. She attributed her plucky character to a grace from 'Jesus, the gentle, little Child of only one hour'[2] at her Christmas 'conversion' of 1886 just before she turned fourteen. It freed her from the hypersensitivity that had afflicted her from the time of her mother's death when she was four and a half years old.

1. *The Story of a Soul,* trans. J. Clarke, Washington, DC: ICS Publications, Washington, 1996, p. 71.
2. *Ibid.,* p. 97.

On the day she received the habit, January 10, 1889, Thérèse would append 'and of the Holy Face' to her name. But the Child Jesus was again prominent. Thérèse had always wished that on that day nature would be adorned in white like her. As if on cue, as she entered the cloister, 'the first thing that struck my eye was the statue of "the Little Jesus" smiling at me from the midst of flowers and lights.'[3] But that was not all. Her glance was immediately drawn to the monastery garden behind it–the garden was covered in snow. For Thérèse it was a thoughtful gift from the Lord: 'Anticipating the desires of his fiancée, He gave her snow. Snow! What mortal bridegroom, no matter how powerful he may be, could make snow fall from heaven to charm his beloved?'[4] This statue was also known as the 'Rose Child Jesus,' and when Thérèse was a new postulant she was given responsibility for it. Her closest sister, Céline (Sr Geneviève of the Holy Face), recalls an incident shortly after Thérèse took charge of it:

> One day she was feeling sorry that she could no longer gather bunches of wild flowers to put at the feet of the statue; she was saying to herself: 'I'll never again see cornflowers, marguerites, poppies, oats or wheat.' That same day the out-sister brought Mother Prioress a gorgeous bunch of all the wild flowers that Sister Thérèse had desired. She had found them on the window sill, and we never found out who had left them there. The event was all the stranger in that the Lisieux Carmel was not as well known then as now, and nobody ever brought us flowers.[5]

A Devotion of Many Forms

Devotion to the divine Infant is a means of honouring Jesus in the mystery of the Incarnation. The Child Jesus has been worshipped in different ways across the world ever since his birth. This adoration continued among Church Fathers and saints in later centuries such as Francis of Assisi, who gave us the crib, and Teresa of Avila. Such is the warmth and universality of this devotion that the Holy Child has been the subject of works by many famous artists, writers and poets. The popularity of the devotion has also given rise

---

3. *Ibid.*, p. 155.

4. *Ibid.*, pp. 155-6.

5. Christopher O'Mahony (ed. & tr.), *St Thérèse of Lisieux by Those who Knew Her: Testimonies from the Process of Beatification*, Dublin: Veritas, 1975, p. 153.

to a wonderful array of statues, sometimes dressed in a variety of sumptuous robes. One nun would report twenty different images of the Child Jesus in her convent alone! Of these, one of the most famous is the Infant of Prague. Maria Manriquez de Lara brought it to Bohemia from Spain when she married Vratislav of Pernstyn. The statue was later given to their daughter, Princess Polyxena von Lobkowicz, as a wedding gift. In 1682, Polyxena, by then widowed, entrusted it to the Discalced Carmelite friars for the benefit of all the faithful. Devotion to the Infant of Prague was then spread throughout the world by the Carmelites. Thérèse stopped to pray each day before a statue of the Infant of Prague close to her cell.

Another popular devotion in France, dating from the seventeenth century, is that of the Child Jesus of Beaune. This devotion is connected with Venerable Marguerite of the Blessed Sacrament (1619-1648), a Carmelite nun who had an apparition which gave her to understand that the Child Jesus wished to be honoured as the King of Kings and Lord of Lords. It was actually before this very statue in the Lisieux Carmel that Pauline (Mother Agnes) suggested to her younger sister Thérèse that she might append 'of the Holy Face' to her religious name.

The Primordial 'Yes'

While Thérèse's love of the Holy Face would become of prime importance to her – 'the foundation of all my piety,'[6] she would say, the month before she died – both devotions still continued as a unity for her. This is reflected in the coat of arms she designed in 1896, depicting both the Holy Face and the Child Jesus. This accord between the two images would have found a ready acceptance at the time. For in nineteenth-century France, to contemplate the divine Infant was to think immediately of the crucified Christ. This is evident in holy pictures of the time, depicting the Infant Jesus with the cross or holding a crown of thorns.[7] The close association of the divine Child with Calvary is found in a favourite contemplation of Cardinal Pierre de Bérulle (1575-1629) – who in fact helped to establish the Discalced Carmelite nuns in Paris.

---

6. *Last Conversations,* Washington DC: ICS Publications, 1977, p. 135.

7. For an account as well as relevant pictures, see Pierre Descouvemont & Helmuth Nils Loose, *Thérèse and Lisieux,* Toronto: Novalis / Grand Rapids, MI: Eerdmans, 1996, pp. 156-63.

This was the primordial 'Yes.' This theme, associated with the French School of Spirituality of which Pierre de Bérulle was the founder, was influenced by a verse in Hebrews, which itself was taken from Psalm 39(40): 'Here I am, I have come to do your will.'[8] In this School, Jesus is seen as offering himself to the Father at the very moment of his conception when Mary uttered her 'Yes' to the Angel. The Cardinal believed that Jesus' entire life was the accomplishment of this original 'Yes.'

On the day Thérèse received the veil, September 24, 1890, she received a holy picture from Sr Marthe to mark the occasion.[9] It depicted, on one side, Jesus in his crib holding a cross; and on the other, the Child Jesus on a cross, with his arms outstretched in self-offering. The first picture is thought to have given Thérèse the idea for her painting *The Dream of the Child Jesus*, in which the Infant Jesus dreams about his future Passion, as shown by a cross and the Holy Face.[10] It is also thought to have suggested to her the idea for the small play she wrote for the community at Christmas 1895, *The Divine Little Beggar of Christmas*, in which all the members of the community are invited to offer their love to the Infant Jesus – to him who is 'the Infant hidden in swaddling clothes… / And who nevertheless can suffer.'[11]

'Word Made Child'

Thérèse's devotion to the Child Jesus endured throughout her life, and in Carmel she delighted in writing plays for the feast of the Nativity. As Céline says: 'it was the Mystery of the Infant Jesus in the Crib at Bethlehem that was her special delight, for it was there that He was in the habit of whispering to her all His secrets about simplicity and abandonment.'[12] In her Christmas play of 1894, *The Angels at Jesus' Manger*, Thérèse was filled with awe at

---

8. Hb 10: 9; cf. Ps 39: 8-9.

9. Eleven years after Thérèse's death, Sr Marthe would detect a delightful fragrance of heliotrope as she passed by the statue of the 'Rose Child Jesus'. She called the then prioress, Mother Marie-Ange, who spontaneously attributed it to Thérèse – upon which the scent vanished: see O'Mahony (ed. & tr.), *op. cit.*, p. 228.

10. In Descouvemont & Loose, *op. cit.*, p. 159.

11. *The Plays of St Thérèse of Lisieux*, trans. S. Conroy and D. Dwyer, Washington DC: ICS Publications, 2008, p. 231.

12. Sister Geneviève of the Holy Face (Céline Martin), *My Sister St. Thérèse*, Rockford, Illinois: Tan Books & Publishers, 1997, p. 46.

the mystery of the God in the crib:

> O God in swaddling clothes,
> You delight the angels.
> Word made Child,
> Trembling, I bow before You.
> Who then will comprehend this mystery,
> A God Who made Himself a little child?...
> He came to earthly exile,
> The Eternal One...the Almighty![13]

This play echoes her encounter with the biblical verse in Céline's notebook which was partly instrumental in the discovery of her spiritual doctrine, The Little Way: 'Whoever is a little one, let him come to me.'[14] She would also often write out a related thought at the end of her life: 'A God who makes Himself so little can only be love and mercy.'[15]

In December 1896, the year before she died, Thérèse wrote a poem, *Child, You Know My Name*. A beautiful, gentle poem, reflecting the paradox of the Incarnation, it portrays her in an imaginary boat steered by the divine Infant who has both a 'sweet gaze'[16] and the power of God:

> With your little child's hand,
>   O what wonder!
> With your little child's voice,
> You calm the roaring waves
>   And the wind! ...[17]

The divine Child may well have actually taken Thérèse on her journey to heaven. On several occasions during her last months, she indicated this expectation. One day, for example, she gazed at a picture of the Child Jesus, depicted as a boy of about ten who was pointing to heaven, and she said: 'It appears to me that this little Jesus here is saying: "You will come to heaven very soon; I'm the one who is telling you!"'[18]

---

13. *The Plays of St Thérèse of Lisieux*, p. 109.

14. Pr 9: 4; cf. *Story of a Soul*, pp. 188 & 208.

15. *The Plays of St Thérèse of Lisieux*, pp. 107-8.

16. *The Poetry of Saint Thérèse of Lisieux*, trans. D. Kinney, Washington DC: ICS Publications, 1995, 42: 1.

17. *Ibid.*, 42: 2.

18. *Last Conversations*, p. 109; cf. pp. 86 & 216.

III
Saint Thérèse, Mary, the Saints, and Spiritual Writers

Chapter Fifteen

The Blessed Virgin Mary in the Spirituality of St Thérèse

'There are preachers who confess that they no longer like to give a sermon or homily on Mary because they are confused as to what they should say.'[1] The confusion referred to here dates from the Second Vatican Council's attempt to correct some flawed types of Marian piety which stem from a centuries old separation between Marian devotion and theology. St Thérèse of Lisieux, however, would have had no such difficulty had she been allowed to deliver a sermon. So dissatisfied was she with some of the homilies she had been hearing that she actually told her sister Pauline (Mother Agnes of Jesus) she would love to have been a priest in order to preach about the Mother of God. She even said that a single homily would have sufficed to teach her message.

St Thérèse not only brought to her Marian devotion a refreshing note of moderation but she also anticipated the very concerns of the Second Vatican Council. In her day there were no shortage of sermons on the Blessed Virgin. Unfortunately, too much emphasis was put on the privileges of Our Lady, keeping her far removed from the day-to-day experiences of the faithful at large. At times, indeed, this lopsided trend seemed to know no bounds.

Mariologists tell us that an authentic Marian devotion requires a balance between two complementary ways of regarding Our Lady. The first approach stresses Mary's privileges such as her status as the Mother of God. We can readily see that a devotion to Mary based on this approach alone would not be a balanced one. We could only admire and venerate the Blessed Virgin but hardly imitate her. The

---

1. M. O'Driscoll, 'Mary in the Christian Life' in *Compendium of Spirituality*, vol. 1, New York: Alba House, 1995, p. 105.

second approach, on the other hand, allows us to see Our Lady's oneness with us. In its attempt to move away from a Mariology centred on the privileges of Mary, the Second Vatican Council emphasised the importance of the latter approach in an attempt to restore a balance. It cannot be stressed too often, however, that both approaches are necessary for an authentic Marian devotion.

As we can see from her deathbed comment to her sister Pauline, St Thérèse was well aware of the need for a balance in Marian piety. It was for this reason that all she had heard preached on the Blessed Virgin left her untouched: 'Let the priests, then, show us practicable virtues! It's good to speak of her privileges, but it's necessary above all that we can imitate her. She prefers imitation to admiration, and her life was so simple! However good a sermon is on the Blessed Virgin, if we are obliged all the time to say: Ah!... Ah! ... we grow tired!'[2] A few days earlier, when she was explaining her ideal sermon on Our Lady, Thérèse told Pauline: 'We know very well that the Blessed Virgin is Queen of Heaven and earth, but she is more Mother than Queen; and we should not say, on account of her prerogatives, that she surpasses all the saints in glory just as the sun at its rising makes the stars disappear from sight. My God! How strange that would be! A mother who makes her children's glory vanish! I myself think the contrary. I believe she'll increase the splendour of the elect very much.'[3]

More Mother than Queen! Thérèse had good reason to feel cared for by the Blessed Virgin. Deprived of her earthly mother when she was only four and a half years old Thérèse made an Act of Consecration to the Blessed Virgin on the day of her First Communion. And it is significant that it was a smiling Blessed Virgin St Thérèse experienced when, she believed, Mary cured her of a strange psychological malady, not the aloof figure who sends the blessed and the angels into hiding. It was also the firm conviction of St Thérèse that it was no mere coincidence that important events in her life, especially those in Carmel, fell on Our Lady's feast days.

She entered Carmel, for example, on the feast of the Annunciation on April 9, 1888, the feast in this year being transferred because of Lent. On her pilgrimage to Rome in 1887, when she

---

2. *Last Conversations*, ed. J. Clarke, Washington, DC: ICS Publications, 1977, p. 166.

3. *Ibid.*, p. 161.

made her dramatic appeal to Pope Leo XIII to be allowed to enter Carmel at the age of fifteen, Thérèse received a special grace, along the way, at the Marian shrine of Our Lady of Victories in Paris, when any doubt about Our Lady's cure was removed. There was, too, the experience she had in July 1889 of being hidden under the Blessed Virgins veil.

We must not infer from these special graces, however, that extraordinary experiences were essential to the Marian devotion of the young Carmelite. On the contrary, in keeping with her general approach to spirituality, she did not seek such gifts but simply wanted to imitate the Blessed Virgin in her ordinary aspect. When, for example, a priest wrote to her expressing his view that the Blessed Virgin did not experience physical suffering she disagreed. She discussed this issue with Pauline: 'When I was looking at the statue of the Blessed Virgin this evening I understood this wasn't true. I understood that she suffered not only in soul but also in body. She suffered a lot on her journeys —from the cold, the heat, and from fatigue. She fasted very frequently. Yes, she knew what it was to suffer.'[4] The centrality of the spiritual motherhood of the Blessed Virgin in the devotion of St Thérèse is nowhere better clarified than in her poem, *Why I Love You, Mary*. Indeed, she told her sister Marie (Sr Marie of the Sacred Heart), 'My little canticle expresses all I think about the Blessed Virgin and all I would preach about her if I were a priest.'[5] It was written in Mary's month, just a few months before she died on 30 September, 1897 at 24 years of age. Significantly, apart from a brief allusion to her miraculous cure, Thérèse dwells on and identifies with the ordinary life and suffering of the Mother of God. This is reflected in Stanza 17:[6]

At Nazareth your life /(O Virgin full of grace!)

Was poor- you didn't long / For comforts not possessed: Did transports, raptures come/Or miracles? No Trace Of these bedecked you there /O Queen of all the blest! Their number's very great/ Your little ones on earth; To lift up fearless eyes I this joy to them is giv'n.

---

4. *Last Conversations*, p. 158.

5. *Ibid.*, p. 235.

6. See *Poems of St Thérèse of Lisieux*, trans. A. Bancroft, London: Fount, 1996, p. 176.

It's by the common way/ (O Mother beyond worth!) That
you are pleased to walk, / To guide them up to Heav'n.

It was, then, to the gospel account of Mary's life that Thérèse
instinctively turned for virtues to imitate. Rather than miracles,
raptures, and ecstasies she found a life of simplicity and humility
totally devoted to Jesus in the service of others. It is these virtues
she extols in her hymn to Mary. The Mariologist Eamon Carroll
points out that when we consider that the idea of Mary being the
first of Christ's disciples is considered to be the dominant truth
emerging from the Gospels' pages among exegetes today we may
indeed gasp with astonishment at just how advanced the interpre-
tation of St Thérèse was nearly a century ago.[7] Moreover, this is
especially evident in the 'true kinsmen' Gospel story[8] which was a
favourite of St Thérèse:

Who is my brother, who / my sister, mother?
He is that, who does my will / Jesus the saviour said.[9]

Many years before *Lumen Gentium* providentially warned against
'false exaggeration' as one of the extremes of Marian piety, Thérèse
had already cautioned against an overstated admiration of Our
Lady. She told Pauline that she would impress upon people just
how little is known about the life of the Blessed Virgin. Our lack
of knowledge about the life of Mary must not, therefore, cause
us to invent. Thérèse warned, 'We shouldn't say unlikely things
or things we don't know anything about! For example, that when
she was very little, at the age of three, the Blessed Virgin went up
to the Temple to offer herself to God, burning with sentiments
of love and extraordinary fervour. While perhaps she went there
very simply out of obedience to her parents.'[10] Thérèse only approved of homilies that allowed her to see the real as opposed to
the imagined life of the Blessed Virgin. She was convinced that
Our Lady's life was very simple. As proof that Mary lived by faith
just like anyone else Thérèse cited the gospel account of the reac-
tion of the parents of the infant Jesus to Simeon's prophecy: 'And

---

7. See E. Carroll, 'Thérèse and the Mother of God', in *Experiencing Saint Thérèse
Today*, Carmelite Studies, Washington, DC: ICS Publications, 1990, p. 93.

8. Mk 3, Matt 11, Lk 8.

9. *Why I Love You, Mary*, Stanza 20, in *Poems*, p. 177.

10. *Last Conversations*, p. 161.

they did not understand the words which He spoke to them.”[11]

In her last days Thérèse suffered greatly. Not only did she have to bear appalling physical suffering, without relief from medication, but she also had to endure the darkness of severe temptations against her faith. During her passion she frequently prayed to her spiritual mother, the Blessed Virgin. Sometimes she was heard repeating the closing lines of *Why I Love You, Mary*!:

> You smiled upon me in / the morning of my life!
> Still, Mother, smile on me! / for it is evening now.
> No longer do I fear/ your blaze of splendour;
> I Have suffered with you. This / I am preparing for;
> To sing, upon your knee/ ‘I love you - listen why’;
> ‘O Mary! I’m your child’ /I’ ll sing for evermore!

Those who read the writings of St Thérèse will have no difficulty preaching or teaching about Our Lady. And now that she has been declared *Doctor Ecclesiae* by Pope John Paul II, they can feel confident about the credentials of St Thérèse of the Child Jesus and the Holy Face as a teacher. In his Apostolic Letter (n. 8), on the occasion of her elevation to Doctor of the Universal Church, Pope John Paul II said, ‘Lastly, among the most original chapter of her spiritual doctrine [The Little Way] we must recall Thérèse’s wise delving into the mystery and journey of the Virgin Mary, achieving results very close to the doctrine of the Second Vatican Council in chapter eight of the *Constitution Lumen Gentium* and to what I myself taught in the Encyclical Letter *Redemptoris Mater* of 25 March 1987.’

Many of us are likely to fear the notion of ever having to give a sermon, let alone one on the Blessed Virgin. This, however, is not the point of the imagined homily of St Thérèse. Her concern was with an unbalanced Marian devotion that prevailed at the time. For Alan Bancroft, one of the translators of her poems, this error stands in contrast ‘with some today who seemingly cannot overstress the “ordinariness” of her who bore God Incarnate.’[12] Bancroft’s comment is a reminder of the constant need for vigilance in our devotion to Mary. Our attempts to observe a more balanced approach to Our Lady in the light of Vatican II and post-Vatican

---

11. *Last Conversations*, p 161.
12. A. Bancroft, trans., *Poems*, p 179.

II developments, in theology and devotion to Mary, need not, however, inhibit our love for her. As St Thérèse told her cousin Marie Guerin (Sr Marie of the Eucharist), 'Have no fear of loving the Blessed Virgin too much, you will never love her enough, and Jesus will be pleased since the Blessed Virgin is his Mother.'[13]

---

13. *Letters of St Thérèse of Lisieux*, trans. J. Clarke, Washington, DC: ICS Publications, 1982, p. 569.

Chapter Sixteen

Saint Joseph in the Piety of Saint Thérèse

The deep devotion Thérèse had to Saint Joseph was only surpassed by her reverence for Mary. The husband of the Blessed Virgin Mary and foster-father of Jesus had a special place in her piety from a very early age: 'Ever since my childhood I had a devotion for him that easily merged with my love for the Blessed Virgin. I recited each day the prayer in his honour.'[1] As a toddler, she would play her part in setting-up the May altar at the family home by happily gathering '…the best roses…the corn flowers and marguerites growing beside the country lanes!'[2] And she kept some of her blossoms '… for St Joseph's statue…'[3]

Thérèse also had an extraordinary reason for her tender devotion to Saint Joseph. Within a few weeks of being born she was snatched from death's door following an impassioned plea to Joseph by her tearful mother Zélie. Two doctors had given up hope of Thérèse's survival from an intestinal disease that had already sadly carried away two of her infant brothers, both of whom were called 'Joseph.'

The wonderful intervention of St Joseph in the Martin home happened at a time of heightened devotion to the saint, a little over two years after Pope Pius IX declared him Patron of the Universal Church on December 8, 1870. Pius IX's declaration was an acknowledgement of St Joseph's power to do good for the Church from his place in heaven. The extent of Joseph's influence is well explained by Basil Cole:

---

1. *Story of a Soul*, trans. J. Clarke, Washington DC: ICS Publications, 1996. p. 124.
2. Stéphane-Joseph Piat O.F.M.,, *The Story of a Family*, Rockford, Illinois: Tan Books, 1994. p. 150.
3. *Ibid.*

...the universal patronage of St Joseph is beneath that of Mary but higher than that of any other saint. To have a ministry relating immediately and directly to the Word-made-flesh is certainly higher than any other ministry save that of being the Mother of God. And since Christ is the head of the mystical body, St Joseph's ministry also extends to all members of the Church and is the fundamental reason why we should honour him in a special way and turn to him in time of need...[4]

When Thérèse followed Pauline and Marie, two of her four sisters, into the local Carmel the place of Joseph in her piety could have found no better environment in which to thrive. Her spiritual mother, St Teresa of Avila, had an exceptionally deep devotion to 'glorious St Joseph' and made him the founder of her reform and monasteries. She also cultivated a devotion to Joseph among her spiritual sons and daughters. In her autobiography, Teresa says of St Joseph: 'I don't recall to this day ever having petitioned him for anything that he failed to grant.'[5] Thérèse alludes to this fact in one of her fifty poems, To Saint Joseph:

> Our Mother, Saint Teresa – who
> Confided in you always – stressed
> She found that when she prayed to you
> Quick answer came to each request.[6]

Thérèse successfully implored St Joseph's powerful intercession on a number of important occasions in her life. She believed, for example, that Pope Leo XIII's relaxation of the rules against the frequent reception of Communion for religious in 1890 was in answer to her petition to Joseph. As a result, whenever she passed his statue she cast flowers at it. Six months before twenty-four-year-old Thérèse died from tuberculosis on September 30, 1897, she was discovered by her eldest sister and godmother Marie (Sr Marie of the Sacred Heart) at the hermitage of St Joseph on his feast day. Marie advised Thérèse that given her poor health it would have been better if she had gone directly to her cell, rather than taking the roundabout route by the shrine of St Joseph. The saint replied

---

4. Basil Cole, 'Universal Patronage of St Joseph' in *Compendium of Spirituality*, Volume 1. New York: Alba House, 1995. p. 117.

5. K. Kavanaugh and O. Rodriguez, trans. *The Collected Works of St Teresa of Avila*, Volume I. Washington DC: ICS Publications, 1987, p. 79.

6. A. Bancroft, trans. *Poems of St Thérèse of Lisieux*. London: Fount, 1996, p. 35.

that she had a specific request for Joseph: 'I am coming to ask St Joseph to obtain from God the grace for me to spend my heaven in doing good on earth.'[7] Marie queried the necessity of having to put this request to Joseph as she had already put the same request to St Francis Xavier at the Novena of Grace earlier that March of 1897. But Thérèse remained adamant that the intercession of St Joseph was essential to her campaign. Céline explains that Thérèse 'seemed haunted with the desire to come back to earth after her death. It was constantly in her thoughts…'[8] This ultimate expression of her desire to become a missionary is reflected in Thérèse being made Co-Patron of the Missions alongside St Francis Xavier, by Pope Pius XI on December 14, 1927.

A century before Vatican II warned against 'false exaggeration' as one of the extremes of Marian piety, Thérèse had already cautioned against an overstated admiration of Our Lady. It was to the gospel account of Mary's life that Thérèse instinctively turned for virtues to imitate. Rather than miracles, raptures and ecstasies she found a life of simplicity and humility totally devoted to Jesus in the service of others. Thérèse's devotion to St Joseph mirrors her tender and balanced devotion to Mary in its avoidance of any sentimentality. Indeed, she understood that the entire Holy Family had, like the rest of us, to cope with the problems of life through the eyes of faith. She therefore preferred to see them in their ordinary aspect and disliked their lives being gratuitously overstated:

For example, that the Child Jesus, after having formed some birds out of clay, breathed upon them to give them life. Ah! No! Little Jesus didn't perform useless miracles like that, even to please his mother. Why weren't they transported into Egypt by a miracle which would have been necessary and so easy for God…No, everything in their life was done just as in our own…How many troubles, disappointments! How many times did others make complaints to good St Joseph! How many times did they refuse to pay him for his work! Oh! How astonished we would be if we only knew how much they had to suffer![9]

---

7. *Letters of St Thérèse of Lisieux*, J Clarke, trans. Washington DC: ICS Publications, 1982. p. 1074, n. 11.

8. Sister Geneviève of the Holy Face (Céline Martin), *My Sister Saint Thérèse*, Rockford, Illinois: Tan Books, 1997, p. 227.

9. *Her Last Conversations*, p. 159.

Thérèse's balanced devotion keeps Joseph close to the ordinary experiences of people: '…And good St Joseph! Oh! How I love him! He wasn't able to fast because of his work. I can see him planning, then drying his forehead from time to time. Oh! How I pity him! It seems to me their life was very simple.'[10] The vicissitudes of Saint Joseph's working life are also taken up in one of Thérèse's eight plays, *The Flight into Egypt*. One of the themes in this recreational piece reflects the awareness she had of a concern with the inequality between rich and poor in late nineteenth century France. As Guy Gaucher explains: 'In the difficulties of Joseph the carpenter we can see the insecurity of the working class.'[11]

Even when Thérèse was on her death bed she could, despite her dreadful suffering, use her imagination to her spiritual advantage. When she was unable to eat and drink the food put before her she would imagine serving it instead to members of the Holy Family: 'St Joseph and the little Jesus have each received a peach and two prunes…The Blessed Virgin had her share too. When I'm given milk with rum, I offer it to St Joseph; I say to myself: "Oh, how much good this will do to Joseph!"'[12]

A few months before she died, Thérèse paused to cast flowers at St Joseph's statue in the garden of the Lisieux Carmel. When she was asked if she was doing so in order to get a special favour her reply reflects the tender affection she had for Joseph: 'Ah! No! I just want to please him…'[13] Given the deep and balanced devotion that Thérèse had for Joseph it comes as no surprise that he too features in her anticipation of heaven in the fifth stanza of her poem, To Saint Joseph:

> And so…till Heav'n our trials here
> Concludes…one joyous hope we share:
> That – with heav'nly Mother dear–
> Saint Joseph, we shall see you there![14]

---

10. *Ibid.*, p. 159.

11. S. Conroy and D. Dwyer, trans., introduction by G. Gaucher, *The Plays of St Thérèse of Lisieux*. Washington DC: ICS Publications, 2008, p. 255.

12. St Thérèse of Lisieux, *Her Last Conversations*, trans. J. Clarke, Washington DC: ICS Publications, 1977, p. 108.

13. *Her Last Conversations*, p. 63.

14. *Poems of St Thérèse of Lisieux*, p. 36.

Chapter Seventeen

Saint Thérèse and Saint Joan of Arc: A Mysterious Kinship

The extraordinary affinity between Thérèse of Lisieux (1873-1897) and Joan of Arc (c. 1412 -1431), even though they lived centuries apart, is reflected in the fact that 'Thérèse wrote more about Joan than she did any other saint ... even to her dying days.'[1] Indeed, so closely associated had they become that Pope Pius XI introduced Thérèse to a group of French pilgrims as 'a new Joan of Arc,' the day after he canonized her on May 17, 1925. Only five years had passed since Joan was canonized by Benedict XV on May 16, 1920. The close affinity between the two young French saints was further underlined on May 3, 1944, when Pius XII gave Thérèse equal status to Joan by declaring her as the secondary patron of all of France.

Thérèse's kinship with Joan began with her love of reading history books as a child of eight or nine. She was particularly attracted to the brave deeds of patriotic women, especially Joan of Arc. She believed her burning desire to imitate them was sent from heaven. Thérèse also received a grace which she considered to be one of the greatest of her life: she believed that she was 'born for glory.'[2] Thérèse's attraction to Joan as a role-model proved to be no mere childhood fancy. However, she was clear from the outset that she would not achieve glory like Joan by marching into battle or being publicly burnt at the stake. Her glory would consist in becoming a saint and her fight would be exclusively on a spiritual plain. Inspired by a picture of Joan, Thérèse prayed:

1. J. Kochiss, *A Companion to Saint Thérèse of Lisieux*. Kettering, OH: Angelico Press, 2014. p. 482.
2. St Thérèse of Lisieux, *Story of a Soul*, trans. J. Clarke. Washington DC: ICS Publications, 1996. p. 72.

O My Beloved! I know what combat you have in mind for
me; the contest will not be on the field of battle…my sword
is nothing but Love! … I will have You proclaimed King in
the souls who refuse to submit to your Divine Power … Joan,
Your chaste and courageous bride said: "We must fight so that
God may give the victory." Oh my Jesus, I will fight then for
your love until the evening of my life…[3]

Thérèse's spiritual fight was realized within the walls of the local Carmelite monastery in Lisieux, a short walk from her family
home, Les Buissonets. However, she increasingly associated herself
with Joan, to the extent that when she looked at her she saw her
own fate as if in a mirror. This is evident, for example, in her poetry and two of her eight recreational plays – *The Mission of Joan
of Arc* and *Joan of Arc Accomplishing her Mission* – where there are
obvious parallels drawn between herself and Joan. The latter is
her longest and most successful play. It is also the work in which
she made an impression in Carmel as an actress. Thérèse's moving
portrayal of Joan took on a somewhat strange aspect when the
stage set accidentally went on fire, leaving the young Carmelite
dangerously surrounded by flames like her heroine. The eminent
Thérèsian scholar, Bishop Guy Gaucher, stresses the importance of
these plays for grasping the profound influence of Joan on Thérèse.

In 1894, Joan of Arc became the focus of an attempt to restore
French pride after the humiliating defeat of France in the Franco-
Prussian war of 1870-1871. When May 8, the date of Joan's lib-
eration of Orléans, was proclaimed a national holiday, a patriotic
and religious fervour swept across France. The drive for the new
annual holiday was led by the efforts of another of Joan's biogra-
phers, Henri Wallon. Thérèse borrowed his biography of Joan from
her uncle, Isidore Guerin, when researching her Joan of Arc plays.
Thérèse's closest sister, Céline, and her cousin, Marie Guerin, both
of whom would soon be numbered among her novices, were busy
making banners to mark the great occasion for their local church
in Lisieux, the Cathedral of St Pierre. Ironically, Pierre Cauchon,
the corrupt leading judge Joan held responsible for her being
publicly burnt at the stake as a heretic, on May 30, 1431, became
Bishop of Lisieux from 1432-1442. Moreover, he is buried in the
Lady Chapel in the apse of St Pierre's Cathedral where Thérèse

3. *The Prayers of Saint Thérèse of Lisieux*, Intro. G. Gaucher, O.C.D., trans. A.
Kane, O.C.D., Washington, DC: ICS Publications, 1997. p. 106.

attended Mass during the week with her father, Louis. Joan of Arc was declared Venerable by Pope Leo XIII on January 27, 1894. From within the cloisters of the local Carmel nearby, Thérèse too got caught up in the national celebratory mood and wrote her first Joan of Arc play to mark the new holiday. She also wrote her fourth poem, *Canticle to Obtain the Canonization of the Venerable Joan of Arc*, for the occasion.

While Thérèse came to prominence on a very different battlefield to that of Joan, her impact on the world was no less astonishing. Devotion to her spread after the publication of her three auto-biographical manuscripts in *Story of a Soul*, after her death from pulmonary tuberculosis on September 30, 1897. In the manner of a great general, Thérèse made the difference by being innovative. Through her celebrated Oblation to God's Merciful Love on June 11, 1895, she was, in the words of Abbe André Combes, '...blazing a new trail of Christian Spirituality.'[4] This became apparent at a time when the icy grip of a residual Jansenism in France was even felt within the Lisieux Carmel. Some of the nuns, for example, would bravely offer themselves as victims of God's justice for the sins of the French Third Republic. But God's justice held no such fears for Thérèse. Although she suffered great anguish from an extreme dread of sin during her early years in Carmel, she came to understand God's love in terms of mercy late in her short life. Indeed, such was her unlimited trust in the mercy of God, and acceptance of her flawed humanity, that her audacious confidence became the outstanding feature of her spiritual doctrine of The Little Way, her greatest legacy to us. Her Oblation to Merciful Love is the symbolic expression of her teaching. She was elevated to the rank of Doctor of the Church by Pope John Paul II on October 19, 1997, only one of three women to be so honoured. Before long Thérèse, who ironically entered Carmel to hide herself from the world, was revered on an immense scale across the globe in so many ways, including the construction of cathedrals, basilicas, shrines and churches under her patronage.

In the last few months of her life, Thérèse struggled to breath with the fraction of a lung left to her, while also enduring her painful and bewildering Trial of Faith. During her suffering, the twenty-four-year-old Carmelite increasingly identified with her

---

4. A. Combes, *The Spirituality of St Thérèse*. Dublin: Gill & McMillan, 1990. p. 47.

nineteen-year-old 'sister' Joan in prison facing death at Rouen. After re-reading her second play about Joan several times, she could see its prophetic character. She confided to her sister Pauline (then Mother Agnès): 'I have re-read the play on Joan of Arc that I wrote...You will see there all my feelings about death; they are all expressed.'[5] Significantly, when shown a picture of herself playing Joan in captivity during her agony it reignited her courage: 'The saints encourage me, too, in my prison. They tell me: As long as you are in irons, you cannot carry out your mission; but later on, after your death, this will be the time for your works and your conquests.'[6] It was becoming clear to Thérèse, then, as her dynamic view of heaven crystalized, that, despite her imminent death, her mission to souls was far from over: 'I feel that my mission is soon to begin, to make others love God as I do, to teach others my Little Way. I will spend my Heaven doing good on earth...'[7]

Over forty years later, while being held captive by the Nazis, Jean Guitton, the distinguished French philosopher and theologian, read and meditated on a book that proved to be something of an epiphany for him concerning Thérèse and her mysterious affinity with Joan. Entitled *From Jesus to Us*, the volume was written by the Russian Orthodox philosopher and poet Dmitri Merezhkovsky (1865-1941), a disciple of Dostoievsky. Guitton was surprised to discover that his Russian counterpart had been compiling a shortlist of saints since Jesus, considered 'to be ranked among the much smaller company of saints of that rare and special degree of insight that can only be called genius.'[8] Coincidentally, the French scholar had already asked himself the same question and arrived at almost the same set of names. He included Joan on his list but not Thérèse. He was therefore surprised to find that both saints were included on Merezhkovsky's list, and that the Russian had chosen the young Carmelite nun as a religious genius 'with absolute assurance.'[9] Merezhkovsky had, interestingly, discerned the same

---

5. *The Plays of Joan of Arc*, Intro. G. Gaucher, O.C.D., trans. S. Conroy & D. Dwyer. Washington DC: ICS Publications 2008. p. 137.

6. *St Thérèse of Lisieux: Her Last Conversions*, trans. J. Clarke, O.C.D. Washington DC: ICS Publications, 1977. p. 144.

7. *Story of a Soul, op. cit.*, p. 263.

8. J. Guitton, *The Spiritual Genius of Saint Thérèse of Lisieux*, trans. F. Leng. Kent: Burns & Oates, 1997. p. 13.

9. *Ibid.*, p. 15.

spirit in Joan and Thérèse and emphasised their extraordinary innovative minds and attitudes:

> ...surely like Thérèse, Joan could have said: "I want to spend my time in Heaven in doing good on earth." Thérèse expressed her religious experience with great precision; Joan lived it out in silence (but more profoundly perhaps than any other saint). They are like each other not only because of a determination to live and act their faith as human beings on this earth, but because they comprise one and the same soul in two bodies...[10]

Finally, while later developing a parallel between Thérèse and Joan in his own book *Problème et Mystère de Jeanne d'Arc*, Guitton says: 'There can sometimes exist certain saints, far apart in history, who form pairs...' And he concludes that 'Joan helps us better to understand the heroism of Thérèse, and Thérèse the simplicity of Joan.'[11]

---

10. *Ibid.*, pp. 35-36.
11. Quoted by Gaucher in *The Plays of St Thérèse of Lisieux, op. cit.*, p. 137.

Chapter Eighteen

Apostles of Divine Mercy: Julian of Norwich and Saint Thérèse

Julian of Norwich, a fourteenth-century English anchoress and mystic, was popular in her own time. After centuries of oblivion, she has re-emerged in recent times to capture an entirely new audience across the denominational divide. Thérèse of Lisieux is, of course, the nineteenth-century French Carmelite nun who has attracted a phenomenal number of devotees across the globe since her death in 1897. The outstanding insights of these two holy women bear a remarkable resemblance in a number of respects, especially concerning the mercy of God. They also share the distinction of having brought hope to the people of God in times of intense anxiety about eternal damnation. The importance of their message about God's mercy has, of its nature, an enduring relevance in any age. It is, after all, the essence of the gospel message. But we would do well not to lose sight of the historical circumstances that gave rise to their thinking. This is all the more necessary since heresies, such as Jansenism, have a habit of re-emerging in various guises in different eras.

Hope in a Grim Century

Julian of Norwich was the only visionary among the late medieval English mystical writers, who include Richard Rolle, Walter Hilton and the author of *The Cloud of Unknowing*. As a result of her visions, she was not only cured of a grave illness, but also completely healed of all anxiety about damnation. An excessive fear of eternal punishment was pervasive among her contemporaries in a grim century when England was devastated by plague, famine, war and corruption. This apocalyptic train of events gave rise to a fixation with penance and release from purgatory. It was evident in wills, bequests and religious practices at the time.

Against this pessimistic background, Julian stands out like a beacon of hope. When all seemed lost, she proclaimed that 'all shall be well.' In her visionary experience, she was overwhelmed by the tender love and condescension of God: 'our God and Lord, so holy and aweful, is so unpretentious and considerate'[1] (R, p.72). She understood that in the endtime, the Blessed Trinity will perform so great a deed that it will iron out all wrongs. In the meantime, she stresses that it is the will of God that we should take humble and serious account of our sin and the harm it causes. But equally, we must, in the course of our ups and downs, have confidence that the abundant divine mercy for us is constant: 'He wants us never to run away from him, whether things are going well or ill.'[2] Indeed, such is the humility and confidence of Julian that she, like Thérèse, approaches Jesus in an attitude of spiritual childhood. This is apparent, for example, in Julian's innovative way of using the then not unusual practice of referring to Jesus as 'Mother':

> But often when we are shown the extent of our fall and wretchedness we are so scared and dreadfully ashamed that we scarcely know where to look. But our patient Mother [Jesus] does not want us to run away: nothing would be more displeasing to him... for when a child is in trouble or is scared it runs to mother for help as fast as it can... And he wants us to copy the child who always and naturally trusts mother's love through thick and thin.[3]

Delighting in her 'extremely friendly' and 'courteous' Lord who assured her that he would keep us all 'safe and sound', Julian asks us to rejoice and trust in the mercy of God rather than sorrowing over our repeated faults: 'Of all the things we may do for him in our penitence the most honouring to him is to live gladly and gaily because of his love.'[4]

Thérèse's Anti-Jansenism

An excessive fear of eternal punishment similar to that of Eng-

---

1. Julian of Norwich, *Revelations of Divine Love*, trans. into modern English by Clifton Wolters, Harmondsworth: Penguin Books, 1966, p. 72.
2. *Ibid.*, p. 198.
3. *Ibid.*, pp. 172-3.
4. *Ibid.*, p. 206.

land in the late medieval period took root in seventeenth-century France because of Jansenism. This gloomy heresy took its name from Cornelius Jansen, professor of scripture at the University of Louvain. Jansenism restricted the hope of salvation to a chosen few. Once the heresy was introduced into France, it soon took hold in the country. Even in the time of Thérèse, a residual Jansenism still maintained a chilling influence on the faithful. Its bleak hold on religious thinking gave rise to an anxiety and fear among God's people about their prospect of salvation. There was a preoccupation with limiting one's stay in purgatory by the accumulation of indulgences and good works, similar to that in Julian's England. But Thérèse did not approve of such a selfish approach to purgatory. The young nun was concerned with the spiritual welfare of others within the entire communion of saints. Although she prayed and made sacrifices for other souls, purgatory came to hold no fear for Thérèse because of her trust in God's merciful love:

> Ah! since the happy day [of my self-offering to Merciful Love], it seems to me that Love penetrates and surrounds me, that at each moment this Merciful Love renews me, purifying my soul and leaving no trace of sin within it, and I need have no fear of purgatory. I know that of myself I would not merit even to enter that place of expiation since only holy souls can have entrance there, but I also know that the Fire of Love is more sanctifying than is the fire of purgatory.[5]

We should also note that, together with Catherine of Genoa, Thérèse has made a crucial contribution to the church by insisting that the correct context for an understanding of purgatory is love.

The influence of Jansenism was even present within the walls of the Lisieux Carmel. It was a custom for some of the nuns to make a heroic offering of themselves as victims to God's justice. Thérèse was largely, though not entirely, spared the ravages of Jansenism because of the influence of the gentle spirituality of Francis de Sales in her family home. While she acknowledged the generosity of her religious sisters, she was not drawn to their approach. Instead, full of confidence in the mercy of God, she made her now celebrated 'Act of Oblation to Merciful Love.'

---

5. *The Story of a Soul,* trans. J. Clarke, Washington, DC: ICS Publications, Washington, 1996, p. 181.

Holiness for Everyone

After a process of trial and error on her spiritual journey, Thérèse came to have an audacious confidence in the mercy of God. Writing to a newly ordained priest, she enthusiastically quotes these words of Psalm 102:

> He is compassionate and filled with gentleness, slow to punish, and abundant in mercy, for He knows our frailty, He remembers we are only dust. As a father has tenderness for his children, so the Lord has compassion on us!![6]

Once she really discovered the nature of God's great self-effacing love and mercy, Thérèse realised that holiness is not only for great souls but is available to everyone. There is one condition, however. We must not resist the grace of God in anything. So, it is not our imperfections that get in the way of divine mercy, but an unrealistic view of ourselves and a false idea of God. Thérèse had made valiant efforts to become perfect. But she did not succeed. It was only when she recognised her inability to achieve holiness by her own efforts that she began to make headway and discover her Little Way. She realised that everything is a grace, that God does all; and that all God looks for in return is a humble recognition of our human weakness, together with a corresponding confidence in divine mercy.

It is this attitude of humility and confidence that opens the way to God's tender and transforming intervention in our spiritual journey. No wonder, then, that Thérèse insisted that confidence in God's merciful love is the only right attitude. She held its omission to be offensive to him. She advised her friend and novice, Marie of the Trinity: 'Hold on tight to your confidence. It is impossible for God not to respond to that, because he always measures his gifts by how much confidence we have.' Thérèse even said that if she had on her conscience all the sins that could be committed, her confidence would not be diminished. It was through the mercy of God that she contemplated all the other divine perfections. She saw even God's justice as clothed in love. As a result, she had no fear. And this was her greatness. But to choose mercy only for its benefits would be to misunderstand the message of Thérèse. It is not an invitation to inactivity. The ultimate proof of Thérèse's

---

6. *Letters of St Thérèse of Lisieux*, trans. J. Clarke, Washington DC: ICS Publications, 1982, p. 226.

love for God was her self-surrender and abandonment to Merciful Love. Such was her confidence that she trusted blindly in divine mercy by accepting in advance whatever life would deliver, moment by moment.

We can readily see how the theological reflections of Julian of Norwich bear a similar healing character to Thérèse's anti-Jansenism for anyone who has been infected with undue pessimism about their fate in the hereafter. We, in modern times, are especially blessed to have Thérèse, one of only three women to be elevated to Doctor of the Church, and to know her transforming spiritual doctrine. In the very first paragraph of Story of a Soul, she speaks of her sole preoccupation: 'I'm going to be doing only one thing: I shall begin to sing what I must sing eternally: "The Mercies of the Lord"'7.

---

7. *Story of a Soul*, p. 13.

Chapter Nineteen

A Window Onto Eternity: Saint Thérèse's Reading of Charles Arminjon

'Now It Is My Turn!'

In May 1887, a new desire for knowledge prompted fourteen-year-old Thérèse Martin to depart from her own rule not to borrow books from her father, and she asked for permission to read a volume lent to him by the nuns of the Lisieux Carmel. The book was called *Fin du Monde Présent et Mystères de la Vie Future* (*The End of the Present World and the Mysteries of the Future Life*) by Canon Charles Arminjon. Thérèse was utterly inspired by what she read, and she shared her new discovery with her closest sister Céline, who was four years her senior.

This volume soon became the focus of their evening conversations by the attic window of the family's summerhouse. When their thoughts turned to heaven, they would repeat to each other a motif which they had adopted from Arminjon's book: 'Now it is my turn!'–words which the author imagines uttered by God and which are explained by what follows: 'The saints have given me the gift of themselves: can I respond other than by giving myself...?'[1] At this point, says Thérèse, it seemed as if she and Céline were 'leaving earth for heaven.'[2] Thérèse compares the graces they had experienced to those given to St Augustine and his mother St Monica at the port of Ostia when, also looking through a window, they were granted a momentary contact with eternal life. As we shall see, Arminjon's volume would influence the shaping of Thérèse's life itself.

1. Charles Arminjon, *The End of the Present World and the Mysteries of the Future Life*, Manchester NH: Sophia Press, 2008, p. 215.

2. André Combes, *The Spirituality of St Thérèse*, Dublin: Gill & Son, 1950, pp. 28-9.

The Right Book at the Right Time

This particular book is not one of the great spiritual classics like *The Imitation of Christ*, most of which Thérèse could recite by heart. On the contrary, had Arminjon's work not had such a profound impact on her, it might well be just another forgotten title by now. Indeed, it has from time to time proved to be a difficult book to acquire: in 1959, for example, the writer Ida Görres lamented the fact that, despite its enormous influence on Thérèse, a copy of this work was not to be obtained.[3] However, an English translation is currently available in paperback, followed in this article and referred to as 'EPW.'

This latest resurgence in interest would surely have pleased the highly respected Thérèsian scholar Abbé André Combes, who believed that Arminjon deserved fame for his work, and indeed the gratitude of the entire Church. On the other hand, Jean Guitton – the eminent scholar, and the only lay person to attend the first session of Vatican II – while acknowledging the book's merits, is not as unqualified in his praise. But his absorbing critique contrasts with that of scholars who merely give Arminjon a nodding mention, or who simply ignore him altogether.[4] Such an omission is one that Combes regrets.[5] Arminjon's volume clearly demands our attention because Thérèse describes her reading of it as one of the greatest graces of her life.[6] Indeed, given its influence on her spiritual formation, we might well agree with Görres' surmise that it falls into that category of works that we call a special 'providence of books'[7] – the right book at the right time. So, what is the nature of this volume? And what effect did it have on the life of Thérèse?

A Lucid Teaching on Eternity

The work was first published in 1881 and comprises nine conferences delivered by Arminjon in the Cathedral of Chambéry in his native Savoy, in the south-east of France, where he was an honorary

---

3. Cf. Ida Friederike Görres, *The Hidden Face: A Study of St Thérèse of Lisieux*, San Francisco: Ignatius Press, 2003, p. 127.

4. See Jean Guitton, *The Spiritual Genius of St Thérèse of Lisieux*, Tunbridge Wells: Burns & Oates, 1997, pp. 91-109.

5. Cf. Combes, *op. cit.*, p. 14, n. 2.

6. *The Story of a Soul*, trans. J. Clarke, Washington, DC: ICS Publications, Washington, 1996, p. 102.

7. Cf. Görres, *op. cit.*, p. 127.

canon. A former professor of Scripture and Church history, also known for his powerful personality, he was in demand throughout France and beyond as a gifted preacher and spiritual director. He was also a friend of the famous missionary Cardinal Lavigerie.

Arminjon was concerned with the erosion of a sense of the supernatural due to the spread of rationalism in France, and with how this trend had undermined a belief in heaven. His sole purpose in writing what he called his 'lucid, clear, and exact exposition, without diminution, of the essential truths dealing with the future life'[8] was to attempt to reverse this alarming situation. His nine conferences are entitled: 'The End of the World: The Signs That Will Precede It and the Circumstances That Will Accompany It'; 'The Persecution by the Antichrist and the Conversion of the Jews'; 'The Resurrection of the Dead and the General Judgment'; 'The Place of Immortal Life and the State of Glorified Bodies After the Resurrection'; 'Purgatory'; 'Eternal Punishment and the Unfortunate Destiny'; 'Eternal Beatitude and the Supernatural Vision of God'; 'Christian Sacrifice, the Means of Redemption'; and 'The Mystery of Suffering in Its Relationship with the Future Life.'

Without Restriction or Measure

Reading this book could hardly have made a greater impression on the youthful imagination of Thérèse. Eight years later, her enthusiasm was by no means diminished as she wrote: 'God found it necessary to join to the "pure flour" [*The Imitation of Christ*] some "honey and oil in abundance" [Arminjon].'[9] And this is how she recalls the profound impact the Canon's conferences made on her:

> All the great truths of religion, the mysteries of eternity, plunged my soul into a state of joy not of this earth. I experienced already what God reserved for those who love Him (not with the eye but with the heart), and seeing the eternal rewards had no proportion to life's small sacrifices, I wanted to love, to love Jesus with a passion, giving Him a thousand proofs of my love while it was possible. I copied out several passages on perfect love, on the reception God will give His Elect at the moment He becomes their Reward, great and eternal, and I repeated over and over the words of love burn-

8. Arminjon, p. xviii.
9. *Story of a Soul*, p. 102.

ing in my heart.[10]

The key parts that touched Thérèse are in Conferences 5 and 7, which we may even say were influential on the future course of her life. From the fifth Conference she copied out a quotation from St John Chrysostom on Divine Love on May 30, 1887, which she would keep in her prayer book in Carmel. Then, on June 4 and 5, she wrote out several excerpts from Conference 7. Arminjon expanded the basic catechesis Thérèse had learned at home and at school, and from reading the Imitation. He not only gave her theological support for her own direction in life, which brought her peace of mind and encouragement; but his overview of salvation history helped her to understand the truths of the faith with an inspiring new vision. In Conference 7, for example, Arminjon draws a picture of the reward in heaven that awaits the saints. This touched Thérèse profoundly, and here we encounter once more the phrase which Thérèse and Céline quoted to each other:

> And the grateful God cries out, 'Now it is my turn!' The saints have given me the gift of themselves: can I respond other than by giving myself, without restriction and without measure?... I owe them more than paradise, more than the treasures of my knowledge; I owe them my life, my nature, my eternal and infinite substance.[11]

Thérèse saw, with a new clarity, that the passing trials and sufferings of this life were a small price to pay for the prize of heaven. Her love for Jesus, which had intensified at the time of her First Communion, became even more fervent. She could not do enough to serve God. And she could not depart soon enough for her eternal destination.

A Zeal for Souls

Thérèse had thought much about eternity from a very young age, and her thinking on the relationship between time and eternity was deepened to a remarkable degree by her reading of Arminjon.[12] He also instilled in her a heightened awareness of how little time we have left to prove our love for God. Thérèse primarily expressed her love by giving Jesus souls. Five months before read-

10. *Ibid.*, pp. 102-103.
11. Arminjon, p. 215.
12. Cf. Guitton, *op. cit.*, pp. 91-109 & 51-8.

ing Arminjon, Thérèse's zeal for souls had already increased at the time of her Christmas 'conversion' after Midnight Mass, with an unprecedented intensity. Céline would testify that Thérèse thought of religious life 'chiefly as a means of saving souls.'[13] And this is reflected in the fact that she toyed with the idea of joining a congregation of missionary sisters, but decided that she could win more souls for Jesus through a life of prayer and self-immolation as an enclosed Carmelite nun.

On May 29, Thérèse sought her father's permission to enter the austere cloisters of the local Carmel. Then, about two months after reading Arminjon, her Carmelite vocation deepened with another grace: while attending Mass with her father, she received a burning desire to save 'great sinners.'[14] Her first success would famously be that of the triple murderer Henri Pranzini. From now on, her desire to save souls grew with each passing day.

'My Desire Is to Work...'

Even among the saints, Thérèse's zeal for souls is outstanding because of her aim to carry out a co-redemptive mission on earth after her death. This posthumous activity not only reflects the limitless desires, which were given her by Arminjon, but also her dynamic view of heaven, which has its basis in the Canon's teaching on angels. Moreover, his description of the terrible events surrounding the wholesale apostasy in the 'end-times' affected her greatly.[15] And the scriptural teaching, that the return of Jesus would not happen until the gospel had been received by all the peoples of the world, left her with a deep awareness of the evangelisation yet to be done. This instilled in her an ardent zeal for the missionary work of the Church. However, in time she would fail to see why her own work on behalf of souls should have to come to an end in heaven. Ten years later, she wrote to the missionary Abbé Roulland

---

13. In Christopher O'Mahony (ed. & tr.), *St Thérèse of Lisieux by Those Who Knew Her: Testimonies from the Process of Beatification*, Dublin: Veritas, 1975, p. 116. Céline specifies that this was Thérèse's view at the age of fourteen, and that when she entered Carmel she also had the special aim of praying for priests and offering herself for the needs of the Church.

14. *Story of a Soul*, p. 99.

15. See Frederick L Miller, *The Trial of Faith of Saint Thérèse of Lisieux*, New York: Alba House, 1998, pp. 100-4.

I really count on not remaining inactive in heaven. My desire is to work still for the Church and for souls. I am asking God for this and I am certain He will answer me. Are not the angels continually occupied with us without their ever ceasing to see the divine Face and to lose themselves in the Ocean of Love without shores? Why would Jesus not allow me to imitate them?[16]

'The Impressions I Receive'

Other sources, such as John of the Cross and most especially the Bible, would in time play their part in the development of Thérèse's spirituality. Although he is rarely mentioned by name as the years go by, the influence of Canon Arminjon is still discernible in Thérèse's writings. There are also echoes of his writing in some of the characteristics of her lyrical style, which she somehow picked up from him and made her own.[17] But most of all, the impact his work made on her as a young girl was still as vivid for her when she thought back to it in Carmel:

This reading was one of the greatest graces in my life. I read it by the window of my study, and the impressions I receive are too deep to express in human words.[18]

---

16. *Letters of St Thérèse of Lisieux,* trans. J. Clarke, Washington DC: ICS Publications, 1982, p. 254.

17. Cf. Guitton, *op. cit.,* p. 95.

18. *Story of a Soul,* p. 102. In *Story of a Soul,* this passage gives the word 'received', implying that Thérèse is looking back at the impact that Arminjon's work had made on her at the age of fourteen. But a recent new edition of the manuscripts of *Story of a Soul* by Conrad De Meester, OCD corrects it (thereby reverting to the 1957 edition of the manuscripts) with the present tense, given above as 'receive' (literally 'feel' – 'ressens': a change from 'ressentais' in the 1992 complete works). This would appear to demonstrate that Thérèse still felt the effects of that reading just as vividly when she thought back to it in Carmel: see Thérèse de Lisieux: *Histoire d'une âme* – Nouvelle édition critique réalisée et commentée par Conrad De Meester, Paris: Presses de la Renaissance, 2005, p. 180, n. 177.

IV
Saint Thérèse, Ireland, and Other Places

Chapter Twenty

Saint Thérèse and Edel Quinn : Spiritual Twins?

One striking aspect of the Venerable Edel Quinn (1907-1944) is the comparison made between the young Irish woman and the great French Carmelite saint, Thérèse of Lisieux (1874-1897). For example, an associate of Edel's in the Legion of Mary recalls: 'A spiritual radiance shone out from her eyes, almost as though streams of light were emanating from some hidden source. There was something in her expression reminiscent of the Little Flower [a popular name for Thérèse], as seen in her best portraits. Now, I can well believe Céline [Thérèse's closest sister], when she tells how one day when they were conversing about the Holy Ghost, and the sacrament of Confirmation, she had to lower her eyes before the dazzling brilliance of those of her sister Thérèse, Edel had something of the same quality. In fact, I had the general impression that Edel and the Little Flower were spiritually twin sisters.. .'[1]

And this was no passing idea. It actually strengthened as the witness got to know Edel even better. Moreover, other people had the same feeling. For example, a Kenyan missionary once observed: 'The way she always smiled and joked about everything reminded me of The Little Flower.'[2]

One important clue to the reality behind this interesting link may be the fact that Thérèse was Edel's favorite saint. Moreover, not only did she read the life of Thérèse carefully but she did so in the original French. An intimate friend recalls:

> Edel had great devotion to the Little Flower. She had a large
> volume of her life written in French; and she used it constant-

1. L. Suenens, *Edel Quinn-Envoy of the Legion of Mary to Africa*, Dublin: C.J. Fallon, 1962, p. 44.
2. *Ibid.*, p. 259.

ly for spiritual reading. Once she lent it to me, I returned it rather soon, as my knowledge of French was not as good as Edel's, and she seemed disappointed. I remember noticing at the time that here and there throughout favorite passages were underlined and had pencil notes in the margin. It seems to have been a well-used book.[3]

Edel's devotion to Thérèse is further reflected in the fact that when she gave her first public talk on the Legion of Mary she held a relic of the saint tightly in her hand to give her courage. It is also noteworthy that Edel went to daily Mass in a local Carmelite convent in Blackrock, a south Dublin suburb, and that her confessor was in the city Carmelite church at Clarendon Street.

This Carmelite dimension to her spirituality would certainly not have been out of place in her role in the Legion of Mary. Its founder Frank Duff was himself a member of the Carmelite Third Order. Notwithstanding the obvious Carmelite influence on Edel, however, it was to the Poor Clares that she turned when she had an early aspiration to enter religious life. But her plans were frustrated by poor health.

Cardinal Suenens observed that these two extraordinary women were cast from identical metal. Apart from having a number of things in common such as wanting to enter religious life from an early age and having a lively sense of humour they both had an audacious spirit. Edel's mother once said of her daughter: 'She never knew what fear was.'[4]

This boldness is reflected in one incident recalled in Cardinal Suenens' wonderful biography of Edel. It is the picture of the young Irish missionary sitting in her broken down dilapidated two-seater Ford in the middle of the jungle, which she jokingly referred to as her 'Rolls Royce,' calmly writing letters while her African driver went for assistance. We may wonder did Edel, who as a legionary was asked to be the child and the soldier of the Blessed Virgin, sense a kindred spirit when she read about the famous audacity of Thérèse. The remarkable daring of Thérèse is not only found in her daily approach to life but is to be found at the very heart of her spiritual doctrine, popularly known as The Little Way. It spread widely throughout the Catholic world shortly

3. *Ibid.*, pp. 57-58.
4. *Ibid.*, p. 8.

after the publication of her autobiographical texts *Story of a Soul* in 1898. The audacity of the young Carmelite nun is nowhere more apparent than in her bold confidence in the mercy of God. At a time when a residual Jansenism, with its emphasis on the severity of God's justice, still beset the Church, Thérèse courageously chose not to follow those, including members of her own convent, who heroically, but misguidedly, offered themselves as victims to divine justice. Their motive was to draw away the wrath of God from sinners. Thérèse had another way in mind in her teaching on the self-acceptance of our flawed nature. She saw the justice of God in a different light: 'even his justice... seems to me to be clothed in love. What a sweet joy it is to think that God is just, i.e., that he takes into account our weakness, that he is perfectly aware of our fragile nature...'[5] She bravely concludes: ' ... What should I fear? Ah! Must not the infinitely just God, who deigns to pardon the faults of the prodigal son with such kindness, be just toward me who 'am with him always' (Lk 15: 31)?[6] The saint's teaching is enshrined in her celebrated Act of Oblation to Merciful Love.

Thérèse had a wise appreciation of the place of suffering in the spiritual life, as did Edel, but it was her self-surrender that eventually took primacy in her spirituality. She was, however, still prepared to suffer joyfully, if it were the will of God, and in fact did so in a manner that leaves us deeply moved. One wonders if Edel, who was never depressed or disturbed by a difficulty, and bravely went to Africa as an envoy of the Legion of Mary, in full knowledge of her poor health, found further strength in the abandonment of the saint from Normandy? Self-surrender in the manner of St Thérèse means accepting in advance, in every detail and circumstance, whatever might confront us in life, be it happy or sad. As with any holy person, Edel's faith was also characterized by self-abandonment to Providence. And as with Thérèse, those who watched Edel in her dying days were similarly impressed by her inspiring self-surrender and holiness. Coincidentally, she like Thérèse also died from tubercolosis.

Whatever their similarities, however, there is one obvious difference between these two holy women. Unlike Thérèse, who

---

5. Thérèse of Lisieux, *Story of a Soul*, Washington, DC: ICS Publications, 1996, p. 180.

6. *Ibid.*, p. 180.

committed an account of her life and spirituality to writing, under obedience as a Carmelite nun, Edel was always careful to conceal her hidden life and had no such demands made on her. A priest in Nairobi wrote:

> It always puzzled me that there was no direct manifestation of the fire that burnt within. She never, in a word or manner, gave any indication of her interior life. The Little Flower, whom she resembled so much, did so. Edel was always perfectly natural and perfectly supernatural. Her humility always impressed me as much as her courage. Archbishop Leen says he watched her closely. I think everybody did. The good she did was due largely to a radiation of her personality. Her influence was exerted by her very presence. I had the impression that she carried about with her some of the heavenly fragrance of Our Lady.[7]

Replying to a close friend who also saw a likeness between herself and Thérèse, Edel wrote: 'I am sure St Thérèse would not be what she is, if she had been in the slightest way like me. You do not know me at all, if you could even for a moment imagine such a thing. You know the Little Flower was a saint, and I am not even on the first rung of the ladder ...'[8]

Notwithstanding Edel's sincere self-effacement, the fact of the matter is she did remind numerous people of Saint Thérèse. Perhaps it is not all that surprising that people made a link between the holy young Irish woman and the French saint. Thérèse had become something of a phenomenon in the Catholic world since her canonization in 1925, when Edel was eighteen. And, of course, even before that great event her fame spread with the publication of her autobiographical texts and her amazing posthumous interventions throughout the world in her *Shower of Roses*. One of these heavenly manifestations happened in Dublin's Strand Street in 1921. A poor gravely ill child with nephritis and dropsy, Laura Fitchett, was instantly healed after 'Blessed Teresa appeared beside the bed and the Blessed Virgin was beside her.'[9]

In 1944, the year Edel died, Thérèse was proclaimed Second

---

7. Suenens, *op. cit.*, p. 242.

8. *Ibid.*, p. 58.

9. St Therese of Lisieux: *The Little Flower of Jesus*, London: Burnes Oates & Washbourne, 1936, pp. 397-398.

Patroness of France, by Pope Pius XII, alongside her favourite saint, Joan of Arc. Edel was declared venerable by Pope John Paul II on December 15, 1994. We pray for the day that she will share something more with her favourite saint when she, too, is canonized.

Chapter Twenty-One

The Dublin Rose

St Thérèse of Lisieux hardly needs any introduction to the city dwellers of Dublin. The saint's popularity was evident in the recent visit of her relics. But it would appear Thérèse made a posthumous visit to Dublin in 1921 to Laura Fitchett, a gravely ill thirteen-year-old child. Having previously come across a brief account of the story in a publication *The Shower of Roses*. Professor Patrick Beecher of Maynooth made a personal and fuller investigation into what he refers to as the Dublin 'Rose.'[1]

The Faith of Mrs Fitchett

In 1925 Dr Beecher traced the family to their home - a single room next to the Holy Faith Convent in Strand Street. The occupants of this poor abode were Mrs Fitchett, her daughter Laura, and Mrs Fitchett's sister, Miss Hennessy. His report tells how <u>Laura was</u> suffering from acute nephritis and dropsy. The

1. Patrick A. Beecher in Thomas N. Taylor, ed., *Saint Thérèse of Lisieux, The Little Flower of Jesus: A Revised Translation of the Definitive Carmelite Edition of Her Autobiography and Letters, together with the Story of her Canonisation, and an Account of Several of Her Heavenly Roses*, New York: PJ Kenedy, 1926, pp. 396-399. Patrick A. Beecher (1863-1940), a noted orator, known for his pungent wit, was born at Tallow, Co. Waterford, Ireland. Having served as a professor on the staff of seminaries in both Canada and the United States, he was appointed Professor of Pastoral Theology, Sacred Eloquence, and Elocution at St Patrick's College, Maynooth in 1904. He was the author of books including *Hints on Reading and Public Speaking* and *The Authenticity of the Holy Shroud*. Beecher personally investigated the cure of a child named Laura Fitchett, interviewing witnesses as well as Laura herself. Previously two Dublin priests had attested to Laura's illness being terminal. Medical attestations had also been provided to this effect. Dr Beecher's account is dated April 16, 1925. Laura fell ill on January 19, 1921 and was cured eight days later, on January 27, 1921. At this time Saint Thérèse was still 'Blessed', her canonisation coming on May 17, 1925.

young child's body had swollen to twice its size. She had gone six weeks without solid food. The doctor had given up all hope, as had two priests. She lay unconscious for three days and was anointed in the expectation of her imminent death. But the girl's mother had not given up hope: "I prayed to Blessed Thérèse, and not only prayed, but cried to her ..."[2] Young Laura got worse, however. She had all the appearance of death. Indeed, Mrs Fitchett, standing beside the bed with her sister and two brothers, could feel no pulse. Naturally they concluded Laura was already dead. One of Mrs Fitchett's brothers put a mirror to Laura's mouth. All was not lost. He declared: "She is not yet dead, as there is moisture on the mirror."[3] But it was all becoming too much for Mrs Fitchett: "I then felt a stifling feeling, and had to leave the room, as I could not bear to see Laura die, and also I had no holy candles, or other things for the wake."[4] But she still had her faith. She made another plea to the Little Flower to send one of her heavenly roses. She then went out for about three-quarters of an hour.

On her return she saw her sister standing at the door. For Mrs Fitchett it was an ominous sign that Laura was dead. She was wrong however. Her sister delivered the amazing news that Laura was cured. When she returned to the room Laura was sitting up in bed looking perfectly well. Not only that, she was making the demands of any normal healthy child, looking for her clothes, wanting to get up, and to be fed.

The Testimony of Miss Hennessy

In her account of the supernatural events that preceded Laura's recovery, Miss Hennessy says that, while she and her two brothers were maintaining a vigil around the bed of the dying girl suddenly Laura felt a thrill passing through her. The child then sat up in bed, joined her hands, said three Hail Marys aloud and bowed her head profoundly at the mention of the Holy Name. Laura's aunt continues: "She then stared at the other side of the bed away from us, and we knew that she was gazing at some invisible person, because her eyes were bright and her whole

2. *Ibid.*, p. 397.
3. *Ibid.*, p. 397.
4. *Ibid.*, p. 397.

face was beaming, and she was drawn in that direction."[5] When one of her brothers spoke to Laura, Miss Hennessy beckoned to him to remain quiet. She goes on: "Next she reached out her hand, apparently in the act of shaking hands, and followed with· her eyes half-way around the bed. Not only did she follow with her eyes, but she was drawn in that direction, and her face was beaming."[6]

Laura's Experience

Young Laura recalls that "Blessed Teresa appeared beside the bed and the Blessed Virgin was beside her. She said: 'Sit up, Laura, and say three Hail Marys in honour of the Blessed Virgin,' and I bowed. She had a lovely white silk bag on her left arm, and she opened it and took out a large white rose and put it to my nose to smell, and then put it back again. Then she shook hands with me, and said: 'Good-bye now, Laura, you are cured.' Then they walked around the bed, and when they came to that spot I couldn't see them any longer."[7]

The Enquiry

When she was being crossexamined about her experience Laura impressed her examiner with her reply, and the manner in which it was given. He was convinced that her testimony was authentic. When asked did the Blessed Virgin say anything to her, Laura replied: "No, but she smiled when I bowed to her." As to the appearance of the Blessed Virgin Mary she said: "She had a blue mantle, but she didn't have any crown." When it was put to her that it was all a dream she answered emphatically "Oh, no, no! It was no dream, I saw her." It was then suggested to her that she was delirious, and that she fancied Thérèse came out of a picture of the saint that hung on the wall. Again the child insisted; "Oh, no, I wasn't. And she was not like any picture I ever saw." When asked to describe Thérèse she replied: "A little girl in First Communion dress, with a white wreath on her head, and she had curls, and a white silk bag on her left arm." Asked did she really feel the hands of Thérèse, she replied that she did. Indeed, Mrs Fitchett reported

---

5. *Ibid.*, p. 397.
6. *Ibid.*, pp. 397-398.
7. *Ibid.*, p. 398.

that Laura was constantly talking about the lovely white hands of the Little Flower. The most convincing evidence was, of course, the fact of the enduring cure itself.

Chapter Twenty-Two

Lisieux and Lubianka: Holiness in Diverse Places

On the face of it, they have nothing in common. One is a pleasant town in Normandy where a saint was nurtured in the local Carmel. The other is a prison in the heart of Moscow, notorious for Soviet torture and executions. One could hardly think of two places more different. Yet, they are associated with two individuals who have left us with inspiring stories of their respective spiritual struggles. One is Thérèse of Lisieux, Doctor of the Church, who needs no introduction to the Carmelite family; the second is Walter Ciszek, a Polish-American Jesuit priest who, for over two decades, experienced Soviet brutality during World War II and the subsequent 'Cold War.' When we compare the stories of these two figures, we soon discover they have much in common.

Striking Comparisons

Walter Ciszek had a burning ambition to become a missionary. Thérèse also had this aspiration. Prior to her sickness, she was giving serious consideration to transferring to the Saigon Carmel. Her solidarity with missionaries is reflected in the fact that, on December 14th, 1927, Pius XI named Thérèse Patroness of the Missions alongside Francis Xavier. While the young Carmelite nun continues to realise her missionary desire in a wonderful posthumous manner by returning to earth 'to make love loved',[1] the story of Walter Ciszek's missionary activity is still extraordinary and immensely inspiring. In the course of their spiritual journey, both Thérèse and Walter had a 'conversion' experience. They both endured intense suffering. And they both had to endure a trial of

---

1. *St Thérèse of Lisieux: Her Last Conversations*, Washington, DC: ICS Publications, 1977, p. 217.

faith. Like Thérèse, Walter Ciszek came to accept the primacy of surrender to the will of God in his engagement with whatever life delivered from day to day. Without prejudice to the unquestionable spiritual genius of Thérèse, there is undoubtedly sufficient convergence between these two figures to link them in a discussion on abandonment to the will of God.

Inspiration in Captivity

Walter Ciszek was exchanged in 1963 for two Russian spies after twenty-three years in captivity. Coincidentally, it was the year Alexander Solzhenitsyn published, in the west, his great novel, *One Day in the Life of Ivan Denisovich*, a story of life in a Siberian labour camp. Ciszek had become a real live Ivan D. For twenty-three years he was held captive by the Soviets, fifteen of them in Siberian slavery. On his return to the United States, he was surprised to hear that he had been officially listed as dead since 1947. He relates his experience in his books, *With God in Russia* and *He Leadeth Me*. By popular request, Walter Ciszek wrote the second of his books for the spiritual guidance of his readers. People wanted to know more detail as to what guided and sustained him during his long captivity in Lubianka and the Communist slave camps.

At the core of this second memoir is a deep religious experience in Lubianka that changed Walter Ciszek's life forever. His brutal Communist tormentors saw to it that he became a broken man. When the Jesuit priest from Pennsylvania signed a false confession that he was a 'Vatican spy', after a year of mental and physical torture, he was overtaken by feelings of unbearable shame and despair. His mental ordeal intensified under this new burden until the spiritual son of Ignatius even lost sight of God. In a moment of blackness all hope had gone. He even felt he had lost his faith. But in the midst of this state of despair, he found that God was not absent after all. Despite his mental turmoil, Fr Ciszek still managed to turn immediately to prayer, to make contact with the God he felt he had forgotten. He prayed that he would never again fail to remember, or to trust in, God. Suddenly, he was consoled by the thought of our Lord's agony in the garden. He identified with Jesus' feelings of fear and weakness there and in particular with his concluding prayer, 'Not as I will, but as thou wilt' (Mk 14: 36). He knew that from then on, he too must live in that spirit of self-abandonment to the will of God.

Humility and Abandonment

Walter Ciszek saw his trust in God in a new light. He had been trying to discern and follow the will of God. But now he realised that:

God's will was not hidden somewhere 'out there' in the situations in which I found myself; the situations themselves were his will for me. What he wanted was for me to accept these situations as from his hands, to let go of the reins and place myself entirely at his disposal. He was asking of me an act of total trust, allowing for no interference or restless striving on my part, no reservations, no exceptions, no areas where I could set conditions or seem to hesitate. He was asking a complete gift of self, nothing held back. It demanded absolute faith: faith in God's existence, in his providence, in his concern for the minutest detail, in his power to sustain me, and in his love protecting me. It meant losing the last hidden doubt, the ultimate fear that God will not be there to bear you up. It was something like that awful eternity between anxiety and belief when a child first leans back and lets go of all support whatever – only to find that the water truly holds him up and he can float motionless and totally relaxed.[2]

Walter Ciszek realised that when he was tested at a critical time, he had a misplaced reliance on himself. It was a lesson in true humility: 'Learning the full truth of our dependence upon God and our relation to his will is what the virtue of humility is all about.'[3] It was this humility that turned him to God and led him to an absolute trust in Providence.

Everything is a Grace

Although the circumstances were obviously different from those of Walter Ciszek, Thérèse also had much the same experience. It was only when she realised her powerlessness, and that everything is a grace, that she began to make rapid progress on her spiritual

---

2. Walter J Ciszek, SJ, with Daniel L Flaherty, SJ, *He Leadeth Me*, London: The Catholic Book Club, 1975, pp. 83-4. [Italics in the quotation are by the author of the article.]

3. *Ibid.*, p. 75.

journey. She came to see that the mercy of God could not be won by means of personal endeavour, no matter how heroic our deeds. She realised that holiness is not about giving but receiving. It is free. And God is both the giver and the gift. She understood that it is only when we realise our utter dependence on our Creator for everything, that progress can be made in the spiritual life. It is then that the Divine Mercy stoops down to help the spiritually poor who seek help with confidence. Céline (Sr Geneviève), one of Thérèse's four sisters, was the most determined champion of her spiritual doctrine, The Little Way. Indeed, she went so far as to assert that it is no longer merely a 'way' because 'by its swift and direct current we are raised like a rocket to the very Heart of God Himself.'[4] Humility, in the sense of recognising our complete dependence on God, was Thérèse's point of departure in The Little Way.

Céline had the privilege of being taught this basic lesson by the saint herself within the walls of the Lisieux Carmel. Walter Ciszek, on the other hand, learned the necessity and meaning of humility in the very different environment of Lubianka prison where cruelty knew no bounds. But once he had absorbed the liberating realisation of his utter powerlessness, it immediately led him to another necessary truth about the spiritual life: the need to live life with a blind trust in divine Providence at each passing moment. In that grim setting, Walter Ciszek changed forever. Thérèse had her 'Christmas conversion' when she was marvellously cured of the hypersensitivity that had beset her since her mother's death. Likewise, Walter Ciszek calls his deep religious experience in Lubianka his 'conversion.'

Conversion in Lubianka

When demanding that he agree to become a Soviet spy in the Vatican, his interrogator found to his dismay and frustration that he was dealing with a new person. Now Fr Ciszek could say:

> My confidence in his will and his providence was absolute;
> I knew I had only to follow the promptings of his grace…
> When at last the interrogator asked me to sign…, I just
> refused… I had simply gone along with everything up to that
> point… He became violently angry and threatened me with

4. Sister Geneviève of the Holy Face (Céline Martin), *My Sister St Thérèse*, Rockford, Illinois: Tan Books, 1997, p.106.

immediate execution. I felt no fear at all. I think I smiled. I knew then I had won. When he called for the guards to lead me away – and I had no assurance but that they were leading me before a firing squad – I went with them as if they were so many ministers of grace. I felt his presence in the moment and knew it drew me toward a future of his design and purpose. I wished for nothing more.[5]

It was in this spirit of abandonment that Walter Ciszek went on to realise his missionary aspiration in the severe conditions of the slave camps in the Siberian tundra. Through it all, finding courage in prayer, he accepted every harrowing moment as God's will, even the relentless, back-breaking fifteen-hour work day–much to the bemusement, and sometimes anger, of his fellow prisoners. In this positive attitude of surrender to adversity, his life's ambition to work in the 'Russian Missions,' for which he was trained, realised itself in an unexpected manner. In the camps he made contact with other Catholics, including priests, and by clandestine means a camp church functioned. Mass was celebrated, sacraments administered, even retreats given. It is no wonder Walter Ciszek extols the virtue of abandonment with an enthusiasm equal to that of Thérèse.

The Abandonment of Thérèse

There was a time when Thérèse identified perfection with suffering. But four years before she died on September 30th, 1897, she revised her definition of sanctity to the doing of God's will.[6] She was still prepared to suffer joyfully, but only if it were the will of God. As things turned out, she did have to endure intense suffering, both mental and physical. And she did so with an attitude of heroic surrender. By then, the priority of abandonment had become a deeply ingrained and all-embracing state in her spiritual life.

Abandonment, in the manner of Thérèse, means accepting in advance, in every detail and circumstance, whatever might confront us in the future. This entails the pro-active reception of whatever one is confronted by in life, happy or sad, at any given moment. It allows no dwelling on the past or worrying about the future. It shuns all introspective self-pity. It also means the rapid

---

5. Walter J Ciszek, SJ, *op. cit.*, p. 88.

6. *Saint Thérèse of Lisieux: General Correspondence*, vol. 2, Washington, DC: ICS Publications, 1988, p. 795.

abandonment of oneself to the merciful love of God in times of moral difficulty, avoiding immediate self-scrutiny or any attempt to confront a difficulty with our own resources. Abandonment lies at the heart of Thérèse's spiritual doctrine, The Little Way. In a letter to Céline a few years before she died, she said: 'I would need a tongue other than that of this earth to express the beauty of a soul's abandonment into the hands of Jesus.'[7]

7. *Ibid.*, p. 850.

Chapter Twenty-Three

Rediscovering Saint Joseph with Saint Thérèse and Saint André Bessette, the Doorkeeper of Mount Royal

In the Life of Thérèse

One day, Thérèse was casting flowers at the statue of St Joseph in the grounds of the Lisieux Carmel, when she was asked whether she was looking for a special favour. She replied: 'Ah, no! It's just to please him; I don't want to give in order to receive.'[1] It is a touching expression of her genuinely tender devotion to 'Good St Joseph.' She recited each day the prayer in his honour and found that her devotion to Joseph easily merged with her love for the Virgin Mary. But we would be wrong to assume from this little episode that Thérèse did not sometimes seek his intercession – she who, at only a few weeks old, had been snatched from death after her mother's impassioned plea to this saint.

There is a notable occasion when Sr Marie of the Sacred Heart was concerned to find the seriously ill Thérèse taking the long route to her cell by way of the shrine of St Joseph. When questioned, Thérèse explained that she had gone out of her way because she needed to ask St Joseph 'to obtain from God the grace for me to spend my heaven in doing good on earth.'[2] Thérèse also dedicated to the saint one of her many poems, which in the final stanza features him in her anticipation of heaven:

And so…until our exile here
Concludes, this joyous hope we share:

---

1. *St Thérèse of Lisieux: Her Last Conversations*, Washington, DC: ICS Publications, 1977, p. 63.

2. *Saint Thérèse of Lisieux: General Correspondence*, vol. 2, Washington, DC: ICS Publications, 1988, LT 221, n. 11, p. 1074.

In Heaven – with our Mother dear –
Saint Joseph, we shall see you there![3]

In Carmel, Thérèse's devotion to St Joseph could, of course, have had no better place in which to thrive: her spiritual mother, Teresa of Avila, had had an exceptionally deep devotion to 'Glorious St Joseph.' I myself now look on this saint as an outstanding example of the interior life and as a role model of all that is decent and good, and so worthy of imitation. All this came to me when I was researching the place of Joseph in the spirituality of Thérèse.

An Unexpected Discovery

Around this time, I happened to make a long-overdue visit to my brother and his wife in Canada. It promised to be the trip of a lifetime. The thought of seeing such creatures as whales and bears, of visiting such wonders of creation as the Rockies, of seeing glaciers, of stepping onto an ice field, induced in me a childlike excitement. But when my wife and I arrived in this vast country, with its friendly and welcoming people, I was more than surprised to find something that would indelibly etch itself on my memory every bit as much as the spectacular vista about us.

A little volume stared me in the face from the bedside pedestal in our hosts' apartment on Vancouver Island. It bore the arresting title, *The Wonder Man of Mount Royal.* Amazingly, it turned out to be the story of a holy man from Quebec who quaintly referred to himself as 'St Joseph's little dog.' He is better known in Canada and the United States than on this side of the Atlantic, and his story was completely new to me. He was a humble doorkeeper called Brother André, famous for his devotion to Joseph and for a multitude of God-given cures, some of them sensational, wrought through his deep devotion to the saint. Not unlike the Curé of Ars, he had to deal with the malign attentions of the devil in various unpleasant manifestations. He is also considered to have had such supernatural gifts as bi-location and of being able to read hearts.

Led to St Joseph

Alfred Bessette–the future Brother André–was born in 1845

---

3. *Collected Poems of St Thé*rèse of Lisieux, tr. Alan Bancroft, Leominster: Gracewing, 2001, *The Poetry of Saint Thérèse of Lisieux*, trans. D. Kinney, Washington DC: ICS Publications, 1995, 14, p. 50.

of humble parents in a small town east of Montreal, now known as Saint-Grégoire. When he was a child, his mother fostered in him a deep devotion to St Joseph. By the age of twelve, he was an orphan. His devotion to Joseph was further strengthened by his parish priest at the time of his first communion. Having worked in labouring jobs across the border in New England for three years, the pious young man returned home. Shortly afterwards, he joined the Congregation of the Holy Cross.

Not only was I completely unaware of Brother André before my trip to British Columbia but, I must confess, I was also ignorant of the fact that St Joseph is the patron saint of Canada. My introduction to the saintly lay brother was not only personally uplifting but it underlined for me the universality of Joseph's patronage, his powerful intercession, and his relevance as a role model. Pius IX declared St Joseph 'Patron of the Universal Church' on December 8th, 1870. Strikingly, it was around this time of heightened devotion to him in the church that the infant Thérèse was cured, after her mother had implored the intercession of Joseph. It was also in the very year of Pius IX's declaration that Brother André, aged twenty-five, was accepted as a lay brother in the Congregation of the Holy Cross–an Order which has always had a special devotion to St Joseph.

Humble Yet Extraordinary

A frail person with little education, Brother André was given the post of doorkeeper at the Order's college. This job also entailed other menial duties, such as waking the community each morning, cleaning, running errands, and collecting the mail each day from the local post office. Altogether, it was an onerous position and he was kept working, day and night, to the point of exhaustion. It was an astonishing workload for someone so fragile and austere. Most of the time, his diet consisted of only a crust of bread dipped in water. He also slept very little. Indeed, his preferred time for praying was at night, in the chapel, when the community were asleep; sometimes it was noticed that his bed had not been touched at all. Wonderful things happened during his nocturnal vigils. On one occasion, while Brother André lay prostrate in the centre aisle lost in prayer, an awe-struck witness saw an apparition in the darkened chapel: he noticed the statue of St Joseph becoming suddenly brilliant and seemingly advancing towards him on a trail of luminous clouds.

It soon became clear that the saintly lay brother had the gift of working astonishing cures in the name of St Joseph. He used these gifts in the service of those who sought his help, especially the poor, the sick and the downcast. Through his extraordinary devotion to Joseph, wonderful cures were wrought. The crippled walked unaided, for example, and the terminally ill were brought back to good health. His chaplain, who was blind, even had his sight restored. Often, people were cured when Brother André rubbed them with St Joseph's oil, from a lamp that was dedicated to the saint in the college chapel.

A Bold Dream

The window of the porter's office looked out onto a nearby hill called Mount Royal. Soon, Brother André became convinced that St Joseph wanted a shrine on the mount. It was a bold dream for someone without money or any earthly influence. But the doorkeeper's confidence came from heaven, where his extraordinary collaboration with Joseph would soon enough unleash a series of supernatural events that would transform Mount Royal into a major place of pilgrimage in North America. St Joseph's Oratory, as it is called, currently attracts some two million pilgrims annually.

When Brother André died on January 6th, 1937 at the age of ninety-one, an estimated million people passed his bier. There is a square named after him in Montreal. In 1978, Paul VI declared him Venerable. John Paul II beatified him in 1982, and during his visit to Canada in 1984 he prayed at the tomb of the extraordinary holy man. Canadians are blessed to have this wonderful shrine to Joseph, their patron saint. But it is, of course, a phenomenon that has universal relevance. Brother André is a model for us all because he imitated St Joseph in his humility. His story can only be of great interest to anyone who has affection for the workman of Nazareth, not least the Carmelite family.

From a Medal to a Shrine

Brother André would advise people: 'Always hold a medal of St Joseph in your hand when making a request, having an interview or transacting an important affair. Holding a medal in one's hand makes one think more of St Joseph than wearing it. Such a practice is proof of great confidence.'[4] Sometimes he would climb Mount Royal to pray. He placed a medal, and later a statue, of St Joseph on the mountain when he was convinced that the saint wanted to be honoured there. The poor lay brother prayed that he would be able to buy a site on the hill for a shrine. Then, after an astonishing sequence of events, his dream was realised. His funds grew slowly, at first with money he earned from doing odd jobs such as cutting the hair of the students, and small donations left at the statue of Joseph by ordinary people.

On March 19th, 1909, the feast of St Joseph, Mass was celebrated at the shrine for the first time. Pilgrims grew in number as news of the marvellous healing powers of the apostle of St Joseph spread throughout Canada and later the United States. However, more important to Brother André than the physical cures were the souls who returned to God. The contributions of those who were cured or who received other favours played an important part in financing his building projects. The initial modest shrine would grow to an imposing basilica.

A Balanced Devotion

It annoyed Brother André when cures were attributed to him. It was in this context that he famously said, 'God performs miracles; St Joseph obtains them. I am only St Joseph's little dog.'[5] Brother André's pre-eminent devotion was not to St Joseph, however, but to the passion of Christ. The author of the little book that awaited me when I arrived in Canada, Henri-Paul Bergeron, was a contemporary and close collaborator of Brother André. Remarkably, he recalls that the lay brother would only occasionally mention the saint in conversation. He would allude to Joseph's perfect obedience and self-surrender in the midst of life's sufferings and joys, but then he would resume his favourite topics: the love and mercy of God, redemption and heaven. But he still maintained a close link between the two devotions. When making the Stations of the

---

4. Henri-Paul Bergeron, CSC, *Brother André: The Wonder Man of Mount Royal*, Montreal: St Joseph's Oratory, 1997, p. 80.
5. L Boucher, *Brother André: The Miracle Man of Mount Royal*, Montreal, 1997, p. 53.

Cross, for example, he seemed to be conversing with St Joseph. Fr Bergeron explains that Brother André's reticence to mention the saint was because his main interest was in imitating Joseph's virtues. The holy man also found himself striving against the ignorance of some people who, unconcerned with living in a state of grace and loving God with all their heart, beg temporal blessings from a friend of God as they would from a politician.

The balanced approach of Brother André is a reminder of the grounded piety of Thérèse whose own devotion to Joseph mirrored her dedication to Mary, in that it avoided any sentimentality. Almost a century before Vatican II, Thérèse warned against false exaggeration as one of the extremes of Marian piety. Referring to the flight to Egypt, for example, she said: 'Why weren't they transported into Egypt by a miracle which would have been necessary and so easy for God. In the twinkling of an eye, they could have been brought there. No, everything in their life was done just as in our own. How many troubles, disappointments! How many times did others make complaints to good St Joseph! How many times did they refuse to pay him for his work! Oh! How astonished we would be if we only knew how much they had to suffer!'[6]

A Hidden Life, a Grand Mission

Brother André, too, had a dread of 'a sentimental spirituality which fosters devotion to the saints but does not trace it to the source of the whole liturgical worship, namely the Holy Trinity, through Jesus Christ Incarnate.'[7] After giving his brief sketch of Brother André, Fr Bergeron regrets that the lay brother did not share the hidden workings of his soul as did 'Little Thérèse'. But, he comments: 'God seems to have reserved for Himself the direction of his spiritual life and to have purposely concealed its beauties, letting only the grandeur of his mission become known.'[8]

My visit to Canada turned out to be more enjoyable than my wildest expectations. Whales were watched, bears were seen, the Rockies explored, and much more besides. But the unexpected 'encounter' with St Joseph, thanks to that modest tome providentially awaiting me on Vancouver Island, will always be gratefully

6. *Last Conversations*, Washington DC: ICS Publications, 1977, p. 159.
7. Bergeron, *op. cit.*, p. 124.
8. *Ibid.*, p. 132.

remembered as a significant intervention in my spiritual life by the loving Creator of all that spectacular natural beauty we were so privileged to behold.

V
Saint Thérèse and the Theatre

Chapter Twenty-Four

Theatre of a Saint: the Plays of Saint Thérèse

A Saint Playing a Saint

Before she ever wrote drama, the acting ability of Sr Thérèse of the Child Jesus became evident in the Lisieux Carmel, when playing lead roles in two of the plays written by her sister Pauline (Mother Agnes): she played St Agnes in June 1888, and the Virgin Mary on Christmas Day, 1889. She performed this last role so well, said Pauline, that 'the Community was profoundly moved and tears poured from every eye. The sisters spoke as one: "Can the Holy Virgin be more beautiful and more heavenly than this?" And this feast day never faded from their memory.'[1] Such was her stagecraft that Thérèse was given the task of composing plays after Pauline became prioress in 1893 and no longer had the time to write them. In all, Thérèse wrote eight religious plays, between January 1894 and February 1897. They reflect some of her most mature spiritual insights. She also acted the leading role in five of her plays. As one might expect from the imagination of a great saint and Doctor of the Church, her involvement with the stage delivered something out of the ordinary, not least the phenomenon of a saint playing a saint.

The theatrical recreations written by Thérèse are the least known of her writings. Because of reluctance on the part of the Lisieux Carmel, they only gradually came to light. In 1910, they had to be submitted for examination, with all her other writings, as part of her beatification process. But the French critical edition, *Théâtre au Carmel: Récréations pieuses* [Theatre in Carmel: Pious Recreations],

---

1. *The Plays of St. Thérèse of Lisieux*, trans. S. Conroy and D. Dwyer, Washington DC: ICS Publications, 2008, p. 17.

did not appear until 1985; and the English translation could not, for various reasons, be published until 2008. Both the French and English volumes contain an excellent General Introduction by Bishop Guy Gaucher.

Portraying The Little Way

Despite the modest nature of this form of theatre, Thérèse's plays have received unstinting praise from one Carmelite author who concludes that what Hans Urs von Balthasar has written about Thérèse's poetry can generally be said of her plays also:

> Though her poetry remains, as to form, a prisoner of the taste of her time—where, after all, would she have learned the language of Péguy or of Claudel?—her mind is a bubbling spring of the most pertinent, the most original and the most unforgettable images which, I am not afraid to say, render her the equal of the two great Reformers of Carmel in poetic power.[2]

There are numerous Theresian themes such as humility, charity and self-surrender, present in her theatrical works. Confidence in the merciful love of God, for example, is evident in several of her plays, including her first Christmas drama, *The Angels at Jesus' Manger*, where the Child Jesus corrects the harshness of the Angel of the Last Judgment.[3] This play also reflects Thérèse's discovery from Proverbs (9: 4), which was partly instrumental in the discovery of her spiritual doctrine, the Little Way: 'Whoever is a little one, let that one come to me.'[4] For the play exemplifies a related thought, which Thérèse wrote out often at the end of her life: 'A God who makes Himself so little can only be love and mercy.'[5] 'O God in swaddling clothes,'[6] she writes in the opening scene, quoting in part from Luke (2: 7). This is just one of the 270 biblical references in her theatrical compositions. And Thérèse could recall many of them from memory.

---

2. John Russell, O. Carm., 'The Religious Plays of St Thérèse of Lisieux', in *Experiencing St Thérèse Today*, Washington DC: ICS Publications (Carmelite Studies, vol. 5), 1990, p. 54.

3. Cf. *The Plays of St Thérèse of Lisieux*, pp. 123-4 & 129-30.

4. Cf. *Story of a Soul*, Washington, DC: ICS Publications, 1996, p. 208.

5. *The Plays of St Thérèse of Lisieux*, pp. 107-8.

6. *Ibid.*, p. 109.

Behind the Scenes

Theatre was originally introduced into Carmel by Teresa of Avila for the relaxation and edification of her spiritual daughters. She sought to ease the strictness of cloistered life on feast days. Writing the recreational pieces was normally the responsibility of the sub-prioress in the Carmel of Lisieux. But when Thérèse entered, Pauline was writing them, having been given the task by the then sub-prioress who felt that she herself had insufficient talent for it. As we have seen, when Pauline became prioress, she handed the responsibility to her youngest sister. This was quite a feat for Thérèse, for throughout 1895–a year in which she wrote three plays–she was also obeying the call from Pauline to write her autobiography. And her free time was limited to one or two hours daily at the most. Thérèse herself asked to play the least important roles but the other sisters, knowing how well she could perform, made sure–five times–that she played the leading role.

Thérèse's plays are, in the main, a mixture of prose and a simple form of verse, which could easily be adapted to the popular melodies that accompanied them. Altogether, her works make use of 26 different tunes. The musical input was helped by her cousin Marie Guérin (Sr Marie of the Eucharist) who entered the Carmel in 1895 and was a gifted singer and pianist. Usually, all the parts were played by the novices. However, they were free to call on the talent of other sisters, especially if they had a good singing voice. When the rapidly maturing Thérèse took over as playwright, she was the *de facto* novice mistress. Around her was a cheerful group of novices. They got an injection of energy from the lively additions of both her cousin Marie and a young new novice who had been a Carmelite in Paris, Marie-Louise Castel (Sr Marie of the Trinity), who would become a close friend. The recreations were mainly staged in the ground-floor 'chauffoir,' the only room in the convent which, as its name suggests, was heated. The novices embraced, with festive enthusiasm, the stage and costume preparations. The trunk of clothes and props in the attic was used in varying degrees, depending on the demands of the play in question–the heroine Joan of Arc, for example, requiring four changes of costume.

Revealing Her Soul

The *Récréations pieuses*, as they are described in the French edition, comprise Thérèse's two plays on Joan of Arc[7]–performed on January 21, 1894 and 1895 respectively; her two Christmas plays[8]–on Christmas Day in those same two years; *Jesus at Bethany*[9]–on July 29, 1895; *The Flight into Egypt*[10]–on January 21, 1896; *The Triumph of Humility*[11]–on June 21, 1896; and *Saint Stanislaus Kostka*[12]–on February 8, 1897. Thérèse's five leading roles were: Joan of Arc,[13] Jesus,[14] Mary,[15] and herself as mistress of novices.[16]

Guy Gaucher says that a prescient dimension to some of these plays became clear to Thérèse's sisters only after she died. It also became evident to the saint herself. She recognised on her sickbed, for example, that a premonition of her mission after her death was evident in the young Jesuit, St Stanislaus Kostka. Thérèse was unable to play this last role because she was too weak from her own terminal illness, and she identified with St Stanislaus who died in 1568 at an extremely young age–just before the age of 18–and who himself was carrying out a posthumous mission. Thérèse confided to Sr Marie of the Trinity: 'What pleased me in composing this play, is that I explained my certitude that, after death, one can still work for the salvation of souls on earth'.[17]

These theatrical pieces also had a purifying cathartic dimension, which allowed the participants to share their talents and express their personalities with a freedom that would not normally be possible. For the playwright, in particular–especially when performing her roles–it meant a certain exposure of her soul that was not demanded by her poetry. Although she used this duty positively, for the benefit of her religious sisters, it must have been a sacrifice for Thérèse who was so intent on the hidden life and on being

---

7. Sainte Thérèse de l'Enfant-Jésus et de la Saint-Face, *Théâtre au Carmel: 'Récréations pieuses'*, Paris: Les Editions du Cerf, 1985, 1 & 3.

8. *Ibid.*, 2 & 5.

9. *Ibid.*, 4.

10. *Ibid.*, 6.

11. *Ibid.*, 7.

12. *Ibid.*, 8.

13. *Ibid.*, 1 & 3.

14. *Ibid.*, 4.

15. *Ibid.*, 6.

16. *Ibid.*, 7.

17. *The Plays of St Thérèse of Lisieux*, p. 332.

'unknown' and 'forgotten.'[18]

'Born for Glory'

The subject of Thérèse's first play was very likely influenced by the then widespread interest in Joan of Arc who was declared 'Venerable' in January 1894, the same week in which the play was performed. But the Maid of Domremy would surely have been of special interest to Thérèse, in any event: Joan was her heroine. Thérèse enthusiastically researched Henri Wallon's vast biography (1877) for her plays on Joan of Arc. Indeed, the second of these was her longest and most successful theatrical work. She had formed an affinity with Joan at the time of her childhood, when she was attracted to books about the brave deeds of patriotic women. And it proved to be an enduring kinship. It was possibly this affinity which gave rise to her warrior instinct and desire to die as a martyr. Thérèse saw in her heroine a reflection of her own destiny: she believed that she, too, was 'born for glory'[19].

Thérèse's own battles, however, would take place exclusively on the spiritual plain. When she became a Carmelite, her identification with Joan of Arc intensified. The eminent French philosopher Jean Guitton calls this a 'mysterious and mystical assimilation' between the two, and he comments: 'There can sometimes exist certain saints, far apart in history, who form pairs or couples. Many of the stars in the sky are double stars...'[20] And on May 3, 1944, the young Carmelite nun from Normandy was posthumously named alongside Joan of Arc as 'Secondary Patron of France.'

A Spiritual 'Holocaust'

As if dramatically to underline her identification with Joan, uncannily the stage-set accidentally caught fire, leaving the actress–just like her heroine–surrounded by flames! The prioress told her not to move, and Thérèse stayed there, 'ready to sacrifice her life.'[21] Guy Gaucher comments: 'Even though she was spared, the flame

---

18. Cf. St Thérèse of Lisieux, *Story of a Soul*, Washington DC: ICS Publications, 1996, p. 152.

19. *Story of a Soul*, Washington DC: ICS Publications, 1996, p. 72.

20. Jean Guitton, *Problème et mystère de Jeanne d'Arc*, Paris: Fayard, 1961, p. 209; quoted in *The Plays of St Thérèse of Lisieux*, p. 137.

21. *The Plays of St Thérèse of Lisieux*, p. 27.

of the bonfire led her unknowingly into a spiritual "holocaust" no less consuming and fierce. An inspiration on 9 June 1895 will find the Carmelite ready to offer herself as "victim" like her sister at Rouen.'[22] Thérèse's absorbing portrayal of her role model is remembered in five photographs taken after the performances by her sister Céline (Sr Geneviève). Shown one of them on her deathbed, she remarked: 'The saints encourage me, too, in my prison. They tell me: As long as you are in irons, you cannot carry out your mission; but later on, after your death, this will be the time for your works and your conquests.'[23]

A careful reading of the plays of Thérèse can yield a rich vein of new information about Thérèse that completes the picture of her other writings. But in order to find what Guy Gaucher calls these 'numerous hidden confidences,'[24] the theatrical recreations must not be read in isolation from the other texts. Interestingly, he cites the Joan of Arc dramas as being the most fascinating examples of where an attentive reader can, with the benefit of hindsight, find these revealing nuggets:

> Without [the Joan of Arc plays], we could not grasp the young Maid of Lorraine's profound influence on the Car-melite and we would have missed the mysterious presenti-ment that dwelled within her as she described the agony and death of her 'dear sister.'[25] She herself only realised this on her deathbed, when she confided in Mother Agnes of Jesus: 'I have read over again the play that I composed on Joan of Arc. You will see there my sentiments about death–they are all expressed.'[26]

22. *Ibid.*, pp. 136-7.
23. *Last Conversations*, Washington DC: ICS Publications, 1977, p. 144.
24. *The Plays of St Thérèse of Lisieux*, p. 31.
25. Cf. *Story of a Soul*, p. 193.
26. *The Plays of St Thérèse of Lisieux*, p. 31; cf. *Last Conversations*, p. 57.

Chapter Twenty-Five

Saint Thérèse and Convent Theatre

Fifteen-year-old Thérèse Martin entered the local Carmelite monastery in Lisieux as a postulant on 9 April 1888. Her sister, 'second mother' and role-model Pauline (Sr. Agnès of Jesus), aged twenty-seven, was the then convent-theatre script-writer and impresario. Writing the plays was normally the responsibility of the sub-prioress but if she did not have sufficient talent the duty was handed over to someone else. Thus, Pauline got involved in writing the theatrical scripts when her sub-prioress did not feel up to the job. In 1893, after her election as prioress, Pauline handed over the closely linked duties of impresario and scriptwriter to Thérèse. But only after eventually conceding that Thérèse could write delightful poetry. Thérèse wrote her first recreation or play, *The Mission of Joan of Arc*,[1] for the prioress's feast day on 21 January 1894. But it would not be until she wrote *Joan of Arc Accomplishing Her Mission*[2] a year later that she made her mark as a playwright, producer and actor, to use conventional theatrical terms. Sr Thérèse of the Child Jesus and of the Holy Face would continue with her convent-theatre duties until her death at twenty-four years of age on 30 September 1897.

Other tasks were asked of Thérèse by the then prioress Pauline. In December 1894, prompted by Sr Marie of the Sacred Heart (Thérèse's eldest sister and godmother Marie), she asked Thérèse to write an account of her childhood memories. This request resulted in Manuscript A, the first of three texts that became the spiritual classic *Story of a Soul*.[3] As with the appointment of Thérèse to

---

1. *The Plays of St Thérèse of Lisieux*, trans. S. Conroy and D. Dwyer, Washington DC: ICS Publications, 2008, 1.

2. *Ibid.*, 3.

3. St Thérèse of Lisieux, *Story of a Soul*, Washington DC: ICS Publications, 1996.

her convent-theatre duties, it could not have been better timed. Thérèse was in the process of discovering her Little Way of love and confidence. Her newfound liberating insights into the merciful love of God, for example, are evident in her second play *The Angels at Jesus' Manger*.[4]

The theatre tradition inherited by the nuns of the Lisieux convent has its origins in the Carmelite reform of their Spanish spiritual mother, St Teresa of Avila, in the sixteenth century. But the roots of convent-theatre are to be found further back still in an ancient monastic tradition. For example, the eighth century English Ecclesiastical historian, the Venerable Bede, alludes to Easter Night theatrical para-liturgies, which were considered at the time to be a means of both education and entertainment.

St Teresa of Avila wanted to introduce a type of theatrical recreation into her convents for the relaxation and edification of her spiritual daughters on certain feast days. Moreover, she was determined that the austere life of her cloistered communities would be lived in a joyful atmosphere. Thus, with a view to avoiding any suggestion of a rigid piety in her convents, she wanted the theatrical pieces to involve singing and dancing. Over the centuries, each of her monasteries developed its own characteristic way of implementing this tradition while remaining faithful to the spirit of its foundress, and very often in outward form as well. Her reform was established in France in 1604 and expanded to Lisieux on 16 March 1838.

The convent plays were intended to mark various liturgical and community feast days, Christmas being the main liturgical feast. In St Thérèse's time, the prioress's community feast was the most important and lasted for over two days; the feast of the Holy Innocents (December 28) was a special day for the novices, when they relaxed most; and the golden jubilee of a nun's profession was also honoured, as were the lay sisters on the feast of St Martha (July 29). As to the nature of theatre at the Lisieux Carmel, the Thérèsian scholar Guy Gaucher says: '…in these enactments of the lives of the saints…a pervasive atmosphere of prayer…makes them far more closely akin to the mystery-plays of the Middle Ages than to mere recreational theatre.'[5]

4. *The Plays of St Thérèse of Lisieux*, 2.
5. G. Gaucher, O.C.D., introduction in: S. Conroy and D. Dwyer, trans. *The*

Pauline wrote six convent recreations altogether and some of her scripts had a lasting influence on Thérèse and her own compositions. Moreover, she gave Thérèse acting roles in two of them: as a postulant she played St Agnès on 21 June 1888, and the Blessed Virgin Mary when she was a novice on 25 December 1889. Her performance in the latter recreation made a profound and lasting impression on the community who were moved to tears.

Long before Thérèse ever became a Carmelite she moved her first audience at the age of four at a school play in Lisieux! The playlet was based on her '…interpretation of *Le Pain de chez nous* (Homemade bread)…'[6] However, her first taste of theatre as a little child was in her family home, Les Buissonnets, where she already exhibited a talent for performance and a special aptitude for mimicry. She inherited these gifts from her father, Louis, who had a fine singing voice and would sing at home and when away on trips. Louis had moved the family from Alençon to Lisieux after his beloved wife, Zélie, died in 1877, in her forty-fifth year (both Louis and Azélie Martin were canonized on 15 October 2015, by Pope Francis). The playlets at the Lisieux home took place in the garden shed which was set up as a children's theatre complete with seats and scenery. There were also roles for Thérèse's siblings and cousins. Pauline, who wrote the scripts, would put into verse the compliments Thérèse, as 'Little Queen', paid to her father on New Year's Day, the feast of St Louis. For Céline, Thérèse's closest sister and confidante, who was four years older, these performances were bittersweet memories. She recalls them with her usual candour which always delighted Thérèse who had a horror of pretence:

> …alas! the childish play was always one with a moral, with good characters and wicked ones. Vice was called upon to throw virtue into high relief and…it was always me in the nasty role! Naturally, we couldn't give such a part to one of our guests. Thérèse was too gentle and kind, since she was queen of the feast, so it was always me, always me.[7]

Plays of Saint Thérèse of Lisieux: Pious Recreations. Washington DC: ICS Publications, 2008. p. 18. Guy Gaucher is uncertain as to whether Thérèse would have approved of the name 'pious recreations'. For example, 'pious' is not part of her normal vocabulary and 'pious conversations fatigued [her] soul'. See p. 50.

6. *Ibid.*, p. 26.
7. *Ibid.*, p. 14.

The ability to compose poetry was essential for writing theatrical pieces because they mainly combined a simple form of verse and prose which could be easily adapted to the popular melodies of the time that accompanied them. Sometimes the plays comprised verse alone. Six of Thérèse's eight plays combine prose and sung verse and she skilfully adapted the words to the different tunes involved. Simple though her theatrical pieces may at first appear, Thérèse put her heart and soul into them. They not only served to entertain but were also intended to teach.

Thérèse wrote eight plays over a period of three years towards the end of her short life. The following list follows the numbering abbreviation RP 1, etc., from *The Plays of St Thérèse of Lisieux*[8] in a modified format:

• RP 1: *The Mission of Joan of Arc* or *The Shepherdess of Domremy Listening to Her Voices* (Performed on 21 January 1894), Occasion: The first feast day of Mother Agnès of Jesus (Pauline) as prioress;

• RP 2: *The Angels at Jesus' Manger* (25 December 1894), Occasion: Community recreation on Christmas Evening;

• RP 3: *Joan of Arc Accomplishing Her Mission* (21 January 1895), Occasion: The feast day of the prioress, Mother Agnès of Jesus;

• RP 4: *Jesus at Bethany* (29 July 1895), Occasion: Feast of the lay sisters (Feast of St Martha);

• RP 5: *The Divine Little Beggar of Christmas* (25 December 1895), Occasion: Community recreation on Christmas evening);

• RP 6: *The Flight into Egypt* (21 January 1896), Occasion: Feast day of the prioress Mother Agnes of Jesus;

• RP 7: *The Triumph of Humility* (21 June 1896), Occasion: Feast day of the prioress, Mother Marie de Gonzague;

• RP 8: *Saint Stanislaus Kostka* (8 February 1897), Occasion: golden jubilee of Sr Saint-Stanislaus (fifty years of profession).

The two Nativity plays RP 2 and RP 5 are thought to have possibly been influenced by Pauline's short play, *The Virtues at Jesus' Cradle*, written some ten years previously.

---

8. *Ibid.*

Written mainly for the novices, the convent plays had a cathartic effect that allowed them to share their talents and express their personalities with a degree of freedom that would not normally be possible in their religious life. The catharsis was that of Aristotle and it extended to all the community who could relate to each other with a greater freedom for the occasion: 'purification of the soul brought on by performance of a play.'[9] The divide between cast and community was not absolute: for example, *The Divine Little Beggar of Christmas*[10] involved all twenty-six members of the community! And the novices were free to recruit the talents of other sisters when needed, especially for singing roles. Another example, Sr Marie of St Joseph had a lovely singing voice and was sometimes included in the cast. Thérèse also filled the role of actor:

> Depending on the genre of the plays, many of the parts could be highly serious. She took the lead role in five of the eight pieces successfully playing Joan of Arc,[11] Jesus,[12] Mary,[13] and her real-life role of "mistress of novices."[14] In RP 2 she also did "the Angel of the Child Jesus."[15]

However, Sr Marie-Madeleine testifies that Thérèse

> …always asked for the least important roles, on the grounds that they were appropriate to her hoarse speaking voice, but we saw to it that she would take the leads that she performed so well.[16]

Joan of Arc Accomplishing her Mission[17] is Thérèse's longest and most successful play, and the work in which she made her finest impression as an actor. Her close spiritual identification with Joan of Arc, despite being separated by centuries, was evident in her portrayal of her heroine. However, the play's first performance took an unexpected turn when a fire broke out on stage and Thérèse found herself surrounded by flames, reminiscent of Joan at the

---

9. *Ibid.*, p. 27, n. 94.
10. *Ibid.*, 5.
11. *Ibid.*, 1, 3.
12. *Ibid.*, 4.
13. *Ibid.*, 6.
14. *Ibid.*, 7.
15. *Ibid.*, p. 26.
16. *Ibid.*, p. 26.
17. *Ibid.*, 3.

stake. The young Carmelite nun narrowly escaped serious burns and could well have died. Despite the danger posed by this uncanny incident, Thérèse did not budge on the orders of the then prioress Mother Agnès (Pauline). In fact, she remained remarkably calm and later recalled she was even ready to sacrifice her life for God. As Guy Gaucher says: 'In such a scene, we are far beyond "mere theatre."'[18] The source of Thérèse's remarkable underlying serenity becomes clear when she was on her deathbed two years later. She was asked by some of the nuns how she could remain so calm in the face of such terrible suffering. Thérèse pointed immediately to her self-abandonment to the will of God, the greatest proof of her love for God and the main stance of her Little Way of confidence and love: 'My heart is filled with God's will, and when someone pours something on it, this doesn't penetrate its interior… I remain always at profound peace in the depths of my heart; nothing can disturb it.'[19]

Two years after *Joan of Arc Accomplishing her Mission* was first performed, and a few months before Thérèse died, she reflected on the play and saw a prophetic dimension in it concerning death and her posthumous mission on earth: 'I have read over and over again the play on Joan of Arc which I composed. You will see there my sentiments on death; they are all expressed.'[20] Moreover, the stage fire incident made another impression on Thérèse: 'Even though she was spared, the flame of the bonfire led her unknowingly into a spiritual 'holocaust' no less consuming and fierce. An inspiration on 9 June 1895 will find the Carmelite ready to offer herself as 'victim' like her sister at Rouen.'[21] This is a reference to St Thérèse's celebrated Act of Oblation to Merciful Love which marked the summit of her spiritual assent. Couched in biblical sacrificial language, the offering has sometimes been misunderstood as necessarily entailing pain and suffering. Thérèse's sister Marie (Sr Marie of the Sacred Heart), for example, was scared to death when Thérèse invited her to become a 'holocaust victim.' However, her mind was put to rest when Thérèse reassured her that the oblation was not a request for suffering. Remarkably, such confusion also

18. *Ibid.*, p. 27.

19. J. Clarke, O.C.D, trans. *St Thérèse of Lisieux: Her Last Conversations.* Washington, DC: ICS Publications, 1977, pp. 97-98.

20. *The Plays of St Thérèse of Lisieux, op. cit.*, p. 137.

21. *Ibid.*, pp. 136-137.

occurred in unlikely quarters: The Liturgical Office of St Thérèse itself had to be corrected four years after it was first published! This amendment followed a complaint from Pauline who was alarmed that the thought of Thérèse had already become so distorted in her own lifetime. She could not rest until the wording 'inflamed with the desire for suffering' was altered to 'on fire with divine love.' Céline helpfully explains how the old biblical terms of the offering find new meaning in the Thérèsian context: 'The new state of the victim she proposed was martyrdom indeed, but a martyrdom of love.'[22] She points out, for example, that the word 'victim' signifies being 'overwhelmed' by a tidal wave of the tender love of God. And 'holocaust' points to being 'burned up' by the divine love.

In his excellent summary of the plays of St Thérèse, John Kochiss brings his expertise as a composer and dramatist to bear on *Joan of Arc Accomplishing her Mission*:

> This is perhaps the best constructed of Thérèse's eight plays. The last pages of the script somewhat resemble opera librettos where music, drama and meaningful lyrics blend, producing a rather impressive, almost operatic finale.[23]

The timing of Thérèse's plays virtually coincided with the welcome addition of three new novices between 1894 and 1895, bringing the number in the novitiate to six. The novices at the time were Thérèse herself, and two difficult lay sisters: Sr Martha of Jesus, who had a bad temper, and Sr Mary Magdalene of the Blessed Sacrament who avoided Thérèse because she feared she could read her soul! Over time Martha grew in her esteem of Thérèse as did Mary Magdalene who, in 1908, prayed to Thérèse for help with a serious leg injury and received a cure. She frankly admits that she was not in a state to profit from Thérèse's guidance:

> ...but since her entry to heaven, I've surrendered the care of my soul to her, and how she has changed me! It's incredible! I'm so peaceful and trusting. I don't recognize myself anymore.[24]

---

22. Sr Geneviève of the Holy Face (Céline Martin), *My Sister Saint Thérèse*, Rockford, Illinois: Tan Books, 1997. p. 80.

23. J. Kochiss, *A Companion to Saint Thérèse of Lisieux*. Kettering Ohio: Angelico Press, 2014. p. 63. See p. 62 for his commentary on RP 3 and pp. 59-66 for his complete summary of the plays.

24. *Ibid.*, p. 343.

The newcomers were all choir sisters. Marie-Louise Castel (Sr Marie of the Trinity), the lively transferee from the Paris Carmel, arrived on 6 July 1894. Although she originally came from the little town of Saint-Pierre-sur-Dives, several miles from Lisieux, Marie-Louise had spent her youth in Paris '...long enough to have kept some of the style of a fashionable young woman of that town.'[25] She was one year younger than Thérèse and became her youngest novice and friend. Thérèse took her new novice Marie-Louise under her wing and helped her overcome numerous difficulties as she adjusted to her new Carmelite home, including a difficulty she had complying with the strict rules concerning comportment: '... posture, glances, movement of feet, manner of sitting, standing, eating, etc.'[26] Thérèse's multi-talented and forthright sister Céline (Sr Geneviève of the Holy Face), entered Carmel on 14 September 1894, having recently refused two proposals of marriage. Céline's many gifts included her extraordinary ability as an artist. She was deemed good enough to study in Paris by her tutor, the highly respected Norman artist, Édouard Krug, with a view to being introduced to its famous Salon and annual art exhibition. Years later, in 1909, she would win the grand prize at the International Exposition of Religious Art in Holland for her painting of the Holy Face. St Pope Pius X was captivated by the beauty of the work. Céline was also adept at the new technique of photography and brought into the Carmel her elaborate 13/18 camera with Darlot lens and accompanying paraphernalia. As a result, Thérèse became one of the most photographed saints in history. Céline's portfolio includes some compelling photos of Thérèse in her role as Joan of Arc. But, most importantly, she brought along her notebooks with passages of Scripture that facilitated Thérèse's inspired discovery of her spiritual doctrine, The Little Way. The third new novice was Thérèse's ebullient cousin and close friend, Marie Guérin (Sr Marie of the Eucharist), who arrived on 15 August 1895, and proved to be instantly popular. Thérèse reports 'the whole novitiate is stricken by contagion...[an] attack of gaiety.'[27] Very intelligent, with a complex personality, Marie had a beautiful soprano singing voice and was also a proficient pianist. She helped to expand Thérèse's repertoire of songs with her own collection of sacred and profane music.

25. *The Plays of St Thérèse of Lisieux, op. cit.*, p. 25, n. 86.
26. *A Companion to Saint Thérèse of Lisieux, op. cit.*, p. 313.
27. *The Plays of St Thérèse of Lisieux, op. cit.*, pp. 25-26, n. 86.

Marie was involved in producing Thérèse's two plays with comic elements: *The Flight into Egypt* [28] and *The Triumph of Humility*. [29]

In preparation for the theatrical productions, the novices would retrieve the impressive range of theatrical costumes and props from the convent attic with festive enthusiasm. They would also joyfully set about such tasks as constructing scenery, painting backdrops, fashioning Joan of Arc's battle standard and sewing costumes. They mainly preferred to stage the productions in the ground floor recreation room – then the only heated room in the monastery! Thérèse would often use her talent for mimicry in the recreation room and lighten the atmosphere for the community. However, because the larger upstairs Chapter Room already had an elaborate set for Nativity plays, built by novices, it is thought likely that *The Angels at Jesus' Manger* [30] and *The Divine Little Beggar of Christmas* [31] were staged there.

A few days before the 1895 Christmas Day performance of *The Divine Little Beggar of Christmas*, a package arrived at the Carmel that contained an important addition to the theatrical inventory. It contained a remarkable gift for the Carmel from Marie Guérin's parents, Isidore and Céline: a wax doll of the infant Jesus. The gift could hardly have represented a greater reflection of the tender devotion that Thérèse had for the Child Jesus: both the lining of the crib and the tunic of the doll of the infant Jesus were lined with swansdown taken from the wedding dress she wore when she received the habit on January 10, 1889. The doll's hair was cut from Thérèse's beautiful tresses when she was a child. [32] The Alençon lace overlay on which the Child Jesus rested was made by Thérèse's late mother Zélie, who ran a business from home as a highly acclaimed lace maker.

The Angels at Jesus' Manger, a play written when Thérèse was at the threshold of discovering The Little Way, was performed during Christmas 1894. The work is a good example of how Thérèse's theatrical recreations reflected her spiritual thinking during the

28. *Ibid.*, 6.

29. *Ibid.*, 7.

30. *Ibid.*, 2.

31. *Ibid.*, 5.

32. P. Descouvemont and H. Loose: *Thérèse & Lisieux*. Dublin: Veritas, 1996, pp. 162-163 for a brief description and photo of the Guérins' gift.

last three years of her short life. The play is filled with awe at the mystery of God in the crib, one of St Thérèse's favourite devotions. For example, two years before she died on 30 September 1897, she would often write out the profound thought that 'A God who makes Himself so little can only be love and mercy.' This beautiful sentiment echoes her liberating insight into the divine mercy that freed her from the great anguish she suffered from an extreme dread of sin during her early years in Carmel. Thérèse's devotion to the Child Jesus is also found in her prayers, poetry and reflections. The play itself is certainly devoid of any sentimentality. As Guy Gaucher notes, *The Angels at Jesus' Manger*

> …has nothing folklorish or dainty about it. It is rather a wonder-filled contemplation that encompasses the entire mystery of the Incarnation, the mystery of self-abasement for love's sake.[33]

In its depiction of the merciful love of God, *The Angels at Jesus' Manger* takes a dramatic turn in the final act. Having stayed silent until the final scene, 'The Angel of the Child Jesus,' one of five adoring angels in the play, performed by Thérèse, speaks out against 'The Angel of the Last Judgement' who struck a terrifying note into the otherwise harmonious dialogues. With sword already raised, the fearsome angel threatens to avenge the ingratitude shown to God. But his strident interjection is defused when the merciful voice of the Child Jesus finally speaks to correct the angel's harshness and to express his tender love for every soul without exception. We hear echoes in The Angel of Judgement's voice of the lingering Jansenism in France, with its bleak fixation with sin and punishment, even among some of the nuns within the walls of the Lisieux cloisters. Thérèse was concerned for these nuns who were in the grip of this extreme teaching. Through the voices of other angels, and there are many in Thérèse's spiritual universe, other themes important to her are encompassed in the play such as her desire for daily Eucharist, her devotion to the Blessed Virgin Mary and the dignity of the priesthood.

The *Divine Little Beggar of Christmas*,[34] in which Jesus begs for the love of each Carmelite, involved the entire community. After an angel lays the divine child in the manger, he sings out a verse

---

33. *The Plays of St Thérèse of Lisieux, op. cit.*, p. 104.

34. *Ibid.*, 5.

from a folded note randomly drawn by each Carmelite with a verse intended to influence her behaviour – be it, for example, a self-gift such as a smile, a song, or a bunch of grapes. The verse is then sung out by a member of the community, on this occasion Sr Marie of the Eucharist (Marie Guérin). When it came to her turn, Thérèse drew the bunch of grapes. She always remembered this experience and it is reflected in the bunch of grapes featured on the coat of arms she designed in 1896.

It is thought likely that the new crib gifted by the Guérins was used again for Thérèse's second longest play: *The Flight into Egypt*.[35] The recreation was performed on 21 January 1896, to mark Pauline's feast day as prioress. While Marie Guérin made an impression with her performances in both *The Divine Little Beggar of Christmas* and *The Flight into Egypt*, the musical boldness of the latter was not to the likeness of Mother Agnès of Jesus (Pauline) despite having been produced to mark her feast day as prioress. She interrupted the play before it was finished! Pauline later contritely explained '…I caused [Thérèse] pain after she had gone to too much trouble to please us, when I told her bluntly that her pious recreations were too long and that they wearied the community.'[36] Pauline had not appreciated the context of the boisterous language of the thieves, who later in the play become believers. It is also thought she may have been fearful of criticism from some of the more rigid sisters in the convent. It is not known for certain when *The Flight into Egypt* was stopped but Céline says it was at the last chant of the Angel. If that was the case it would have been an unfortunate interruption that deprived the play of its meaning. Afterwards, Céline happened to come across Thérèse in one of the alcoves secretly wiping some tears away, '…then regaining her self-control, she remained peaceful and sweet in spite of the humiliation.'[37] As a result of the fiasco, Thérèse remained true to her inspiring humility by obediently curtailing the length of the last two plays: *The Flight into Egypt* and *St Stanislaus Kostka*.

Thérèse wrote her last play, *Saint Stanislaus Kostka*,[38] to mark the golden jubilee of Sister Saint-Stanislaus on 8 February 1897.

---

35. *Ibid.*, 6.
36. *Ibid.*, p. 254.
37. *Ibid.*, p. 254.
38. *Ibid.*, 8.

Sr Saint-Stanislaus (Marie-Rosalie Guéret) was the oldest member of the community and Thérèse's infirmarian. She was born in Lisieux on 4 May 1824 and 'participated in the foundation of the Lisieux Carmel…'[39] Thérèse was assistant to Sr Saint-Stanislaus in the sacristy from 10 February 1891 to 20 February 1893. There was a warm mutual affection between the two and the latter called Thérèse her 'little daughter.' Apart from being asked to write the play for Sr Saint-Stanislaus's jubilee by the then prioress Mother Marie de Gonzague, Thérèse was not altogether unfamiliar with the name of Saint Stanislaus Kostka. When she entered Carmel in 1888, the cell she was first assigned was dedicated to him. The striking parallels between the inspiring life of the Polish Jesuit, who also died young and had a premonition of a posthumous mission, helped Thérèse find words to articulate her own increasing desire for a posthumous mission on earth. She confided to her youngest novice, Sr Marie of the Trinity (Marie-Louise Castel):

> What gave me the most pleasure in composing this piece is that I've expressed my certainty that, after death, we can still work for the salvation of souls on earth. St Stanislaus who died so young, has given me a way to speak about my thoughts and my aspirations about this.[40]

Ironically, because of Thérèse's advanced pulmonary tuberculosis it is thought likely that she was too ill to perform. And, because she was 'a little deaf,' it is not known if seventy-three-year-old Sr Saint-Stanislaus was able to enjoy the play.

The theatrical scripts of St Thérèse were the least known of her writings because they were only gradually released into the public arena over a long number of years due to a reticence on the part of the Lisieux Carmelites to do so. In his General Introduction to *The Plays of St Thérèse of Lisieux: Pious Recreations*,[41] Guy Gaucher says:

> Undoubtedly, the Carmelites of Lisieux lacked the free spirit of their Spanish foundress and hesitated to reveal the existence of their innocent recreations to the public; similarly, many years later Sr Geneviève [Céline] still opposed the publication of photographs of her already 'disguised' sister as

39. *A Companion to Saint Thérèse of Lisieux, op. cit.*, p. 334.
40. *Ibid.*, p. 332.
41. Sainte Thérèse de l'Enfant-Jésus et de la Saint-Face, *Théâtre au Carmel: 'Récréations pieuses'*, Paris: Les Editions du Cerf, 1985.

Joan of Arc.[42]

Even when the prospect of Thérèse's beatification loomed and all the writings had to be gathered together, Mother Agnès (Pauline) still believed she should not release certain poems and recreations that she considered trivial and unworthy of the notice of the judges. The net result of these undoubtedly well-intended delays is that the public was only made aware of three actual 'theatrical pieces' in 1929–four years after Thérèse was canonized! And it would not be until 1985 that the French critical edition of St Thérèse's plays was eventually published by Cerf, *Théâtre au Carmel: 'recreations pieuses.'*[43] Thankfully, ICS Publications in Washington DC, who had already done so much to publish other major works of St Thérèse in English, mainly translated by the late John Clarke, OCD, opened-up the plays to the English-speaking world with their English translation of the Cerf publication in 2008: *The Plays of St Thérèse of Lisieux: Pious Recreations*[44] which was translated by Susan Conroy and David Dwyer.

The fact that St Thérèse has since become a Doctor of the Church further reinforces the importance of everything she wrote – including her theatrical scripts. As Guy Gaucher points out, Thérèse's plays cannot be isolated from her other writings:

> We have noted that they complete each other. If we are to make a synthesis, we must include every piece of the puzzle provided by the saint's various works.[45]

---

42. *Ibid.*, p. 45.
43. *Ibid.*
44. *The Plays of St. Thérèse of Lisieux.*
45. *Ibid.*, p. 33.

Chapter Twenty-Six

Christmas at the Theatre of Saint Thérèse

St Thérèse's portrayal of the Blessed Virgin Mary in a Nativity play on Christmas Day 1889 made a big impression on her religious sisters. Moved to tears, the nuns of the Lisieux Carmel could hardly have been more glowing in their praise of the young novice's performance: "Can the Holy Virgin be more beautiful and more heavenly than this?"[1] After Thérèse died, the older members of the community preferred to hold on to the enchantment of that treasured memory rather than allow it be blurred by watching someone else in the part, "because they had felt they could see the Blessed Virgin herself in the form of the angelic novice..."[2]

Convent-theatre was introduced by St Teresa of Avila in the 16th century for the relaxation and edification of her spiritual daughters on feast days. The compelling acting of Thérèse brought to this modest form of drama a profound spiritual quality. In time she would be asked to write her own play scripts. Her total output of eight theatrical recreations included her two Nativity works: *The Angels at Jesus' Manger* and *The Divine Little Beggar of Christmas*.

Thérèse put her heart and soul into her recreational pieces. She used them not only to entertain but also as a vehicle to share her unfolding spiritual insights. Her plays, however, are the least known of her written works because they were only gradually released into the public arena over a long number of years. The welcome English version of *Théatre au Carmel: Récréations pieuses* [Theatre at Carmel: Pious Recreations], with a very helpful General Introduction by Thérèsian scholar Bishop Guy Gaucher, and quoted herein, was published in 2008.

1. *The Plays of Saint Thérèse of Lisieux*, trans. S. Conroy and D.J. Dwyer, Washington DC: ICS Publications, 2008, p. 17.
2. *Ibid.*, footnote no. 57.

Writing the convent plays was normally the responsibility of the sub-prioress. But if she did not have sufficient talent the duty was handed over to someone else. Thus, her sister and role-model Pauline (Sr Agnes) got involved in writing the theatrical scripts when her sub-prioress did not feel up to the job. When she was elected prioress in 1893 Pauline gave the duty to Thérèse, mainly because she recognized her youngest sister's increasing talent for writing poetry. The ability to compose poems was essential for the writing of theatrical pieces. The plays mainly combined a simple form of verse and prose which could easily be adapted to the popular melodies that accompanied them. Sometimes the recreations comprised verse alone, as with *The Divine Little Beggar of Christmas*.

Pauline asked Thérèse to write her first Nativity play in 1894. Thérèse already delighted in writing verse to the Child Jesus and her devotion was nowhere more evident than before the manger: "...it was the Mystery of the Infant Jesus in the crib at Bethlehem that was her special delight, for it was there that He was in the habit of whispering to her all His secrets about simplicity and abandonment..."[3] Thérèse received numerous graces from the divine Infant, including a "singular favour" when she was waiting to enter the convent: she mysteriously anticipated the religious name that was chosen for her by the Carmelites–Thérèse of the Child Jesus.[4] However, the grace that most informed her devotion to the Infant Jesus, and her associated contemplation of the Incarnation, was her Christmas "conversion", after she returned home from Midnight Mass in 1886, when she was freed in an instant from the crippling hypersensitivity that had afflicted her since her mother's death: "... the gentle, little Child of only one hour...made me strong and courageous..."[5] Moreover, as Guy Gaucher points out, Thérèse knew that the Child Jesus who had freed her was "the strong and powerful God"[6] she had received at Mass. Indeed, "Everything concerning the Child Jesus confirms that Thérèse's concept of the Incarnation owes nothing to any lukewarm sentimentality, romancing on the frailty of the newborn in his crib."[7]

3. Sister Geneviève of the Holy Face (Céline Martin), *My Sister Saint Thérèse*, Rockford, Illinois: Tan Books & Publishers, 1997, p. 47.

4. *Ibid.*, p. 71.

5. *Story of A Soul*, trans. J. Clarke, Washington DC: ICS Publications, 1996, p. 97.

6. *Ibid*, p. 98.

7. *The Plays of St. Thérèse of Lisieux*, p. 34.

The Angels at Jesus' Manger was performed in 1894, and *The Divine Little Beggar of Christmas* in the following year. Both performances took place in the evening after Christmas dinner. Significantly, the former quotes Proverbs (9: 4), a key text which was partly instrumental in the discovery of her spiritual doctrine The Little Way: "Whoever is a little one, let that one come to me." The plays were written specifically for novices, but sometimes they felt free to call on the help of other sisters, especially someone with a good singing voice. The theatrical pieces had a cathartic affect on the novices, allowing them to share their talents and express their personalities with a freedom that would not be normally possible in the course of their religious life. The novices would retrieve the impressive range of props and costumes from the convent attic with festive enthusiasm and set about constructing the sets mainly in the ground floor *chauffoir*, which as its name suggests was the only heated room in the Carmel. However, because the upstairs Chapter room already had an elaborate crib built by the novices, it is thought likely that both of Thérèse's Christmas recreations were staged there.

A touching lyrical contemplation on the paradox of the Incarnation, *The Angels at Jesus' Manger* reflects Thérèse's wonderment at the loving self-abasement of God in this great mystery and is already evident in the opening refrain:

> O God in swaddling clothes,
> You delight the angels.
> Word made Child,
> Trembling, I bow before You...[8]

This play has six characters. In addition to the Child Jesus - who remains silent until the final scene - there are five adoring angels: 'The Angel of the Child Jesus' (played by Thérèse); 'The Angel of the Holy Face'; 'The Angel of the Resurrection'; 'The Angel of the Eucharist' and 'The Angel of Last Judgement.' With dramatic effect the Angel of the Last Judgement strikes a terrifying note into the otherwise harmonious dialogues when, with sword already raised, threatens to avenge the ingratitude shown to God. But his strident interjection is defused when the merciful voice of the Child Jesus finally speaks to correct the angel's harshness and express his tender

8. *Ibid.*, p. 109.

love for every soul without exception.

We hear echoes in the Angel of Judgement's voice of a lingering Jansenism within the Lisieux Carmel. Thérèse was concerned for certain nuns who were in the grip of this bleak teaching and its perverse fixation with the justice of God. Through the voices of the angels, a number of other themes important to Thérèse are encompassed in the play such as her devotion to the Blessed Virgin Mary; her desire for daily Eucharist and the dignity of the priesthood.

Why should this play marking the joyful feast of the Nativity include an Angel of the Holy Face? This may seem odd to us today given that the image of the Holy Face denotes the adult suffering Jesus with a crown of thorns. However, it was not so in 19th century French popular devotion: to contemplate the divine infant was to think immediately of the crucified Christ. This union between the crib and the cross is explicitly seen in holy pictures of the period where the Child Jesus is sometimes shown carrying a crucifix, or indeed stretching his arms out on a cross. Thérèse had a number of such pictures in her collection.[9]

The Divine Little Beggar of Christmas involved all 26 members of the community. The play, in which Jesus begs for the love of each Carmelite, opens with a short sung preface in which an angel appears among the gathered community carrying the divine little beggar.

> Oh my sisters, approach without fear.
> Come, each in your turn.
> Offering your love to Jesus,
> You will know His holy will.
> I will tell you the desire
> Of the Infant hidden in swaddling clothes[10]

The Mother Prioress is first to approach the crib and adores the divine child whom the angel has laid in a manger. The angel then hands the Prioress a small basket filled with pieces of paper from which the Prioress randomly draws one. Without opening it the Prioress hands the folded sheet to the angel. When unfolded, each

---

9. See *Thérèse and Lisieux*, Pierre Descouvement (Text) & Helmuth Nils Loose (Photography), Toronto: Novalis; Dublin: Veritas, and Grand Rapids: Eerdmans 1996, pp. 156-157.

10. *The Plays of St. Thérèse of Lisieux*, p. 231.

note reveals a verse intended to influence the behaviour of the particular nun. The angel sings aloud the alms in whatever form the Child Jesus suggests, be it a self-gift such as a smile, a song or a bunch of grapes. After kissing and caressing the Baby Jesus the Prioress returns to her place and each nun, in order of rank, repeats the routine. When it came to her turn, Thérèse drew the bunch of grapes:

> My sister, how sweet is your fate!
> You are this chosen Grape.
> Jesus will press you very strongly...[11]

It was an experience she always remembered and is reflected in the bunch of grapes which features on the coat of arms she designed in 1896.

After the nuns return to their place, the play ends when the angel takes the Infant Jesus in his arms and sings the concluding verses.

The play encourages the sisters as to the worthiness of the various aspects of their religious life. But it is also a call not to store up good works and merits, a mistake Thérèse once made herself, but simply to give Jesus the one thing he asks for—our love.

---

11. *Ibid.*, p. 236.

RECOMMENDED CARMELITE WEBSITES

For more information about the Carmelites today, our spirituality and our ministries worldwide, visit:

The Carmelite Order:
ocarm.org

Province of the Most Pure Heart of Mary:
carmelites.net

Center for Carmelite Studies at Catholic University of America:
carmelites.info/CenterForCarmeliteStudies

Carmelite Institute of North America:
carmeliteinstitute.net

For a listing of Carmelite provinces worldwide, visit:
carmelites.info/provinces

For a listing of Monasteries of Carmelite nuns, visit:
carmelites.info/nuns

For a listing of Carmelite Hermitages, please visit:
carmelites.info/hermits

For a listing of sites about Lay Carmelites:
carmelites.info/lay carmel

For a listing of Affiliated Congregations and Institutes:
carmelites.info/congregations

For our work with the United Nations, visit:
carmelitengo.org

For more information about publications, visit:
carmelites.info/publications